13/11/15

To:

Darling Ernesto... I hope
supports you on your.

Much love to you and Michael ...
from Anton xx & Poppy °°°° xx

A GIFT
OF HOPE

P.S. Heather Malow
is my great friend xx

A GIFT OF HOPE

DAILY WORDS FROM THE SILENCE

COMPILED BY HEATHER MARLOW

Swift publishing

DEDICATION

To my late parents Florence and Phillip Searle
To whom I owe everything

Swift Publishing Ltd,
145-157, St John Street,
London,
EC1V 4PW

First published by Swift Publishing in September 2015

ISBN: 978-0-9927154-7-2
ebook ISBN: 978-0-9927154-8-9

ACKNOWLEDGEMENTS

To receive encouragement is a wonderful gift. So I thank you all. It would take another book to mention everyone by name, so if you do not find yourself here, you know who you are.

Firstly to Tim and all at Swift Publishing, you have turned a daunting task into a pleasurable one.

Eleanor O'Hanlon for proofreading the manuscript and giving me the confidence that this book should and could be printed.

Josephine Wayne, for our time sitting together and for introducing me to the late great Ursula Roberts, and everyone who I have sat in circle with.

All of my yoga and spiritual teachers, and students both past and present, who helped open the doors to my awareness.

And to all of my family. To my sister Robin, who gives so much love. We are the reason that the telephone was invented. To my husband Jeffrey, children, Gregory, Sophie and Maggie for being there every step of the way. Your love and support is a true blessing.

TESTIMONIALS

These daily meditations come as a blessing and a gift from the inner space of silence where the restless mind is stilled and we know peace. These words have the penetrating simplicity of truth and authentic inner experience. Each line unfolds on the gentle, harmonious rhythms of the breath, and the heart opens and sings as we sense the sacred Presence at the core of our being.

For me, this book has been like a beautiful companion that I could trust and turn to at any point whenever I needed words of truth to still my mind and guide me back into the peace of that Presence. There is profound wisdom and sure guidance on the path in these pages, and a pure light that gives hope and helps us through the challenges of the every day. Above all, there is the assurance of Love as the very essence and foundation of all, the most precious of all gifts, freely given and received with every breath.

This book speaks simply and directly of universal truth, beyond the forms of belief. In a crowded book market, I believe that *A Gift of Hope* has the potential to appeal to the many readers who are searching for direct inner connection and the authentic experience of peace.

Eleanor O'Hanlon, author of 'Eyes of the Wild Journeys of Transformation with the Animal Powers'. (2014 Nautilus Gold Books Award for Nature Writing.)

This book of daily meditations is a work of true inspiration, written from the heart, which invites the reader to open their own heart and go deep within. *A Gift of Hope* is a wonderful companion to daily meditation practice, as it gently and surely guides the reader out of the thinking mind, into the stillness and silence of the centre, the place of true love, from which all life flows.

These meditations are gateways to the deeper levels of our being, which become obscured by the thought streams in the mind that we identify with. In words that are simple, lucid and direct, Heather opens the way to the true peace that is ever-present within us. As we enter inner space, stillness and silence, we find rest. And there we also find connection with the whole of life and realize that life is multi-dimensional and has immense depth.

I warmly recommend this book as a companion to meditation practice, and a beautifully direct and simple guide to conscious presence and connection in daily life.

Steve Pope BD MA, author of 'Patterns of Creation Logos and The Tree of Life in the Gospel of John'.

'A Gift of Hope' reminds us of something we all have, if we care to look, invite and receive it. Heather Marlow's uncluttered words of wisdom, love and hope, clearly and simply suggest that we do indeed have a propensity for a way of being that takes us beyond ourselves.
If we can get out of our own way for long enough a quality arises that may, until now, have been buried beneath a veneer of conditioning. Heather Marlow's insights, emerging from her own patient and effortless practice are an inspiration for those of us interested in loosening the bonds of habit and fear. Her words touch the heart and her observations clear the way for our own interpretation of an alternative intelligence.

Hope is a gift, and Heather Marlow's gift to us is to help us remember how we can see ourselves, and life, in an alternative light.

John Stirk, International yoga teacher and author of 'The Original Body'.

FOREWORD

Dear Reader,

You are the "Now."

While every day life moves quicker and quicker around us it is hoped that the words in this book can help you re-remember your true potential and the joy and harmony of peace.

This book can be read daily or opened at any page to discover the message within that speaks to you directly of hope and encouragement.

Some may use the writings as an inspiration for the day, or for others it may answer a silent question that has been with them for some time.

Each one of us is special and unique and so the words will hold a different meaning for whoever reads them.

A Gift of Hope has no dogma or denomination and it speaks to people of any, or no spiritual path at all. The words come directly from the inner space of peace, connectedness and love, beyond labels and concepts, and they gently guide the reader to encourage mindfulness in daily life, so that they may know themselves as they really are.

It is a companion for Inner Peace.

Thank you for sharing your time with me.

Heather Marlow

Beyond all actions
Beyond all words
Beyond all thoughts
Is the supreme Silence.

It is in this Silent Space
That the potential of all is held
The Unity of life is realized and experienced.

Therefore be still.
Let all thoughts settle.
Know your breath
And with Love
Move deeper into Self.

This will allow you
To understand and melt into the Whole
Bringing Peace and Wisdom.

Practice with Joy and Patience
For only in time will this gateway open to you
Shining Light on you as you move forward
Allowing you to blend into all of Creation.

JANUARY

1ST JANUARY

It is the first day
Of your New Year
For you measure time in light.
Yet you do not know the true meaning
Of such a measurement.
Ask yourself:
"What is light?
And what does it truly mean?"
Surely light is what matters in your world.
Each of you should consider
Bringing light and sharing it with all
For light comes from your Heart
And each life span is measured
In how much light is brought to others.
So stop
And ask yourself:
"Can you bring more?
What needs to be done?"
And in a loving way
Begin to implement the changes.
Move slowly with Love
Surrounding yourself and spreading
The Light of Love to all.

Blessings to all.

2ND JANUARY

It is Now:
There is no other time or place
But this.
For this Now
Will lead you into your future.
Therefore think carefully
On how you wish to experience your time
Then act upon the Now
For this moment holds all things.
It is your past and your future
All in the one moment
Thereby allowing you the choice
Of how you wish to be
And what it is
That you will become.
Think well on this
Then act accordingly.
Know these words to be True:
"For only you plant the seeds
Which makes you responsible
For all in your life."
So go slowly with Love
Spreading light to all
Thereby bringing Peace and Harmony
To yourself and those around you.

                                        Blessings to all.

3RD JANUARY

To begin again
Is not in the future.
It is in the Now.
Therefore each second
Holds the potential
For positive change.
This happens when awareness opens
And allows a constant
Here and Now.
Only with practice
Can this occur
For the individual is filled
With smaller self
Thereby holding unnecessary thoughts.
By letting go of smaller self
And concentrating on the True Self
Change will eventually happen.
Therefore let go.
Open to Love.
Let its light fill
And fulfill you
And experience each wonderful moment
As the future unfolds before you.

                                    Blessings to all.

4TH JANUARY

It is a very positive mind
That can always think
Of goodly things.
Yet to re-remember
Is of the utmost importance
For it only takes a breath
To re-connect with your centre.
This can be done in a second
And from this you will
Reap many benefits.
By doing so you can help
Not only yourself
But also others.
So silently take time to breathe
And unite with your Higher Self
Thus bringing a Blessing to all.
For this surely is your life's work
To bring Peace and happiness
By spreading Love and Light.
Remember and be glad that sometimes
You return to your natural being.
Treasure these moments
Until they spread to hours and years
Of Loving Kindness to all.

Blessings to all.

5TH JANUARY

Why rush?
For in doing so
You move further away
From your still centre
And it is from there
That true consciousness begins.
In the Stillness
Is all that ever was
Or will be.
So by losing your connection to Self
You distance yourself
From uniting with the Whole.
Therefore - stop - wait
And slowly reconnect
So that you can experience
The vital threads of Being.
Look - listen - feel
And you will re-remember
All that is
Thereby opening your Heart to Love
And sending a Blessing
To the world around you.

Blessings to all.

6TH JANUARY

How can you Love others?
By seeing them as yourself.
Yet do you truly Love yourself?
Surely you have been told
To think of others first
Therefore it may seem strange
To ask you to Love
And show Compassion for self.
Yet this is what is asked.
For here is the difference:
It is for your Higher Self
To show the way to Love others.
By recognizing your self
And the Higher Self in others
You can immediately understand
The need for loving self.
Experience each effort
Self has made
Then having true Understanding
You will Love yourself
And others
With your whole Being.

Blessings to all.

7TH JANUARY

To live your life fully
You must first know
Who you really are
For you are more than the outer shell
Or the material objects that you own
Or the labels that others place upon you.
You are indeed
More than all these things.
It is your deep Self
That holds your True existence.
It is for your learning
That you are here.
By developing your Inner Being
You will at last begin to grow
And have an Understanding
Of the reason for your presence on earth.
So look deeply with Love
For Love holds the key
To your Life
And by sharing Love with others
You will allow
A Divine Light to shine forth
Enabling you to flourish
And you yourself
To become a Gift for all.

Blessings to all.

8TH JANUARY

What is the difference
Between right and wrong?
And how do you know it?
The answer is simple:
Let all come from Love.
For actions motivated
By true Love
Can only lead to an Understanding.
Therefore look to your deeds.
If there is only Love
In your Heart
Without any self gain
Then there is a freedom of giving
That can be accepted
If not acknowledged.
So ask yourself
The simple question:
What amount of Love
Is in your actions?
Then when you know
Proceed with a giving Heart.

Blessings to all.

9TH JANUARY

There are things that can be known
And others that cannot
While with others you may get
The slightest hint.
So ask yourself
What is it that you really
Want to know?
Could it be your ego asking
Or is it the true yearning
Of your Heart of Hearts?
For if it is the latter
Then surely with time
And contemplation
You will discover the answer.
The yearnings of the Inner Being
Are filled with Love
And Love will always be answered.
Yet know this to be True:
"That all questions receive answers
Yet they may not be the desired ones."
So think carefully before inquiring
And be prepared for the Truth.

Blessings to all.

10TH JANUARY

Be still.
In a world of constant movement
Allow that you understand Stillness.
For only then
Can you experience the Inner Silence.
It is from there
That all comes
Yet it is not at some
Far distant place
Rather it is deeply within your Self.
Know this to be True:
" To know others
You must first know yourself."
The meaning of this
Is to have experienced
The Stillness of Being
And in doing so
Acknowledge the Unity of All.
This will enable you to share Love
Even with those who you
Normally not do so.
Yet by sending a silent thought of Love
It will be received in the same way
Thus spreading Love and Light
Around your world.

Blessings to all.

11TH JANUARY

When you seek help
Look around you.
Take comfort in the knowledge
That others like yourself
Are on their own pathway.
Therefore each one of you
May find life difficult sometimes.
Yet it is said:
"You are given
That which you require to grow
And none of it is too much for you
To deal with efficiently."
While at the time these words
May seem impossible to hear
And bring irritation
Nevertheless they are true.
So for help
And Inner strength of Being
Contact your Higher Self
Which will allow you Peace
And a calmness and clarity of mind.
This will enable you to proceed
With Loving Kindness for all
And you yourself will have the ability
To grow and move forward.

Blessings to all.

12TH JANUARY

Look around you at nature.
See how things change
Yet remain the same.
Therefore to create change
The best approach
Is to move slowly
For with rushing into things
There is little time for thought
And even less time
For others to adjust.
So to be certain
That you are moving
In the correct way
Take your time.
Ponder on your reasons.
Then slowly move
Into your chosen space.
Do so with Compassion
And Love for all.
In this way acceptance is sure
And a Blessing of Grace
Will be given.

Blessings to all.

13TH JANUARY

Although outer appearances
Are important
What truly matters
Is what is in your Heart.
Therefore look deeply.
Face that which you see.
Then with Love
Begin to change.
For if you yourself
Find it hard to do so
You will understand
How much harder it is
For those who do not
Know of these words.
Therefore deal kindly
And with Love to others
Realizing that indeed
Change must happen
Even when it is not wanted
And events are held onto.
The choice is whether
To make life easier or not
For change will occur.
So flow with the natural rhythm of life
Thereby bringing Love to all.

Blessings to all.

14TH JANUARY

Time passes.
What do you show for it?
How do you measure your Life?
Is it by possessions
The outer trappings of self?
Or by the way others think of you?
For surely there is more to you.
So when you are alone
Still and silent
You can meet and recognize
Your True Self.
It is then
That you can review your life.
By facing your Inner Being
You will learn the Truth.
So wait without judging.
Look with Love and Compassion.
Understand and know
That all passes
And change occurs
With or without your Blessing.
Therefore be kind
To yourself and others
Allowing your pathway
To unfold as it should.

Blessings to all.

15TH JANUARY

The energy of the earth and heavens
Is within you.
There is no difference
Between you and all of the universe.
You are all made of the same matter
And all exists by the breath of Life.
Therefore look to all
As your family
Whether it be in human form or another
For Life is Life
And all should be regarded as such.
Remember this when you deal with your surroundings
So that Respect and Understanding
Mingled with Love are given by you.
This will enable you to melt
Into the Oneness of the Whole
And by doing so
Reach a state of Wisdom and Compassion
Which is the goal
Of your earthly existence.
Know these words to be True:
"From the smallest
To the largest
You are all One."

Blessings to all.

16TH JANUARY

What are your fears?
Do they have grounds for reality?
Or are they based on your imagination?
And do they stop you
From being yourself?
So stop.
Be still
And ask yourself
How do you wish to live?
Either in fear or Love?
Usually the latter is chosen.
Yet how to implement the change?
It is by taking the time
For Inner Stillness
That you will find the strength
To bring this about.
With this comes the realization
That you are truly Loved
And by knowing this
You will blossom into Self
Thus being able
To give Love and Compassion silently
Thereby surrounding yourself and others
In the glow of Harmony and Peace
Bringing Light to the world.

Blessings to all.

17TH JANUARY

In each life tears will fall.
Yet liken this to the nourishment
Of the earth
If the plant is to grow.
Therefore look towards each shower
As part of your growing process.
In this way
You will not be caught up
In each situation
But will seek to find
The reason behind it
And having done so
All meaning will go deeper
And you will have
Greater Understanding
So that you may
Reach your goal
And learn how to live
In the ways of Truth and Light.

Blessings to all.

18TH JANUARY

From this day
Look towards your words.
Let none escape
That may do harm
Or bring pain.
For such is the power
That each utterance
Is of vital importance
Not only to your growth
But also to your world's.
Therefore be at Peace.
Allow others their foolishness
As at times you have had yours.
Know that with Stillness
All things are possible
And what is required
Will come to pass
At the right time
In the right way.

                                    Blessings to all.

19TH JANUARY

Each day is a fresh beginning
Giving you the opportunity
To start again.
By looking back
You may leave behind
All unwanted thoughts and behaviour
Allowing you to go forward
With that which you require.
So look no further for change.
Do not fret about the past
For you have a choice
Whether to move onward
With Hope and Love
Into a new future
Or to remain locked in your old ways.
This is up to you.
So sit quietly and decide
For once a step is made
No matter how small
Help will be given.
Have Faith.
Be courageous
Knowing help is at hand.

                                    Blessings to all.

20TH JANUARY

Flower petals in a storm scatter
Yet the beauty
Of what they were
Remains in your Heart.
So it is
With the frailer things of Life
They were not meant to last.
Yet the stronger
More meaningful things
Will remain with you
To add to your strength.
In this way
You will know what is right.
So go with the natural flow.
Let what must pass do so.
Bless them
With all of the Compassion you possess
And let them go on their way
Making your encounter
A beautiful memory
Held within you.

                              Blessings to all.

21ST JANUARY

Take what is rightfully yours
No more - No less.
In this way you will
Be able to walk though life
Disturbing as little as possible.
For yours is a silent journey
Working towards your goal
Encouraging those who wish it
And sending Compassion
To those who do not understand.
Therefore send a Blessing to all
Knowing that all will take place
At the right time
In the right way.

                                        Blessings to all.

22ND JANUARY

It is Light
That makes the difference
Between being able to see or not.
In Light all darkness goes
And the brighter and higher
That the Light emanates from
The fewer shadows remain.
So even in the darkest of times
Look upwards.
Allow the Light to penetrate
Deep into your Being.
Then let it radiate
To all who wish to receive
Its loving rays
For as you give
So your ability
To receive increases
Thereby allowing you
To become a vessel
Of Compassion and Understanding.

Blessings to all.

23RD JANUARY

At this time
There seems to be
Much sorrow and confusion.
Therefore people need
Strong encouragement
Not only to take on great tasks
But to deal with
The slings and arrows
Of daily life.
For each one
Shall in their own way
Be given that which will help.
Ether by the written word
Or by a friendly voice
They will find
Comfort and support.
This is the purpose of this book:
For each to read
And then share
With Loving Kindness
So that all may be helped
Along their pathway.

Blessings to all.

24TH JANUARY

Allow each individual
To express themselves in a way
That is right for them.
Therefore have patience with others
That they may see the Light
In their own time
For what is right for you
May not be correct for others.
With these words in mind
Think on everyday matters
And see how each one struggles.
Some go forward
Others stay in the same place.
Yet each one is as important
As another.
Therefore look with eyes
That hold Compassion for all.
Understand that a silent Blessing
Filled with Love
Is the most precious of Gifts
That you can give
And do so gladly.

Blessings to all.

25TH JANUARY

There are ways in which
You may go about your life
That make as little disturbance
As is possible.
That means helping
Not too little
Not too much.
In this way
You are Being
Instead of Doing.
The fine line that is drawn
Allows people the opportunity
To develop for themselves.
One therefore has to be like a good parent
Who shows then reminds
But knows that all must
Make their own way
And learn from any mistakes
Just as they themselves had to
In the School of Life
Sorting through each situation
As it arose.
Therefore send Love silently
Knowing that this in itself is sufficient.

Blessings to all.

26TH JANUARY

Where is the beginning?
Or the end?
For the road you travel
Is endless.
Therefore do not look
At how far you have reached
For in that way
The ego lies.
Yet be willing
To continue
To awaken your own awareness
Thus being able
To send Love to others
When it is required.
This is the way
Of true unfoldment
And a greater understanding of reality
Allowing you to cope
With Life's lessons.
Go forward.
Be resolute in your conviction
That Love holds the meaning of all.

                                    Blessings to all.

27TH JANUARY

Today is a time for Stillness.
It is for you to listen
To your Inner Self
To find peace
And quiet within.
For too long now
You have been moving too quickly
And although you have been told
You have not yet taken note.
Therefore now you must be still
So sit erect
Breathe deeply
For in this way
True Understanding
Of Light and Love
Shall be reached.

                                        Blessings to all.

28TH JANUARY

Where do you rush to now?
Yet the world has gone on regardless
Without you yourself
Being instrumental
In its events.
Therefore before you once again
Begin movement
Think twice
Upon what is really necessary.
Use yourself wisely.
Allow each movement
To become more concise
Thereby saving your energy
For what is truly important.
In this way
You will be able to send
Love and Light
In a wider radius
Bringing Peace to many.

Blessings to all.

29TH JANUARY

To help others
You must first help yourself.
Therefore know what is within your Heart.
Look towards your own Truth
For how else can you be of use
If you have not discovered
Your secret mind?
At first there is nothing there.
Then dislike
Then fear.
This is the true darkness
Which is necessary to know
So that you may wash away
All of the impurities.
Then you will be free
To rise upward.
So look closely.
Do not pretend.
Search.
Go forward to the Light
And let Love
Wash over you.
In this way
All shall be given
At the right time.

                                    Blessings to all.

30TH JANUARY

From deep within you comes a stream of Light.
Even in the darkest times
This Light emanates constantly.
It is always there.
Let it fill you
Embrace you
So that you realize
That you are never alone.
Always fulfilled
Always loved
Always cherished.
Let this remind you
Who you really are.
Therefore be content
And allow your life
To gently unfold as it will.

Blessings to all.

31ST JANUARY

Come see how things are done.
Look around you
And decide how you wish to be.
The choice is in your hands
Either to be part of the Whole
Or separate from each other.
There is no time like the present
For a major change in self.
Know that change is coming.
So go forward willingly
In Peace and Love
Which will allow you
To travel your pathway
With its obstacles and pleasures
Always choosing Life
For yourself and others
Especially for those you Love.

Blessings to all.

FEBRUARY

1ST FEBRUARY

Go now
For what you seek to find
Has not been hidden from you.
There is no great secret.
All is Love.
How can there be anything else?
Look around you.
What is missing?
Surely it is Love.
This simple thing Love
Holds the world together.
When it is gone all falls apart.
So walk and in your own way
Spread Love
Even if it is silently
By a smile
A tender look
Or touch.
This will bring Joy into the world.
Go now.

Blessings to all.

2ND FEBRUARY

Each day can either bring joy or sorrow.
It is how it is looked at
That can make the difference
Between an acceptance of life
Or a battle that brings great pain.
When trouble falls
It is easy to move into doubt and fear.
Yet with an overview of life
Patience and calm
Can allow a strengthening of ability to cope
With whatever comes.
Therefore take heart
And realize that great lessons
Can and will be learnt
With the attitude of Love
For this brings greater Understanding
Of the flow of Life.

Blessings to all.

3RD FEBRUARY

Is it easy? – No.
Should it be? – No.
Then you might ask: why?
Rather ask: what is the purpose of life?
Surely it is to grow
To understand the meaning of humanity.
Look around you
And then realize
That you are part of the Whole.
Not separate.
Not special.
Only special when all is One
And you can truly say
You care for and Love each other.
Look to yourself
In your Heart of Hearts
And work towards that answer.

                              Blessings to all.

4TH FEBRUARY

Find a quiet place and be still.
Breathe gently
And let your awareness open.
Rise upward and unite with Love
Letting it flow through you
And around you.
Melt into Love
So that you yourself
Become Love
And smiling inwardly
Blend with the Peace and Joy
That is your True Self.

Blessings to all.

5TH FEBRUARY

Once again come from your Heart
For where else is there to radiate from?
Even when you are uncertain
Look no further
Than the true Centre of your Being.
From there comes the Truth.
Even if at first flow the thoughts of self
When all has settled
The Truth will remain
And you will come to understand
The actual reality.
From there you will act accordingly
Allowing all to be at Peace.

Blessings to all.

6TH FEBRUARY

Let all uncertainty fall away.
What was
Becomes what is
And what is
Was once what was.
Look therefore not backwards
But strive for going forwards.
In each Heart
There is the possibility for change
So from where you are standing
Go forward.
Gather all that you wish to become
And leave behind that which is negative.
Have hope in your Heart.
Open and let the Light of Love burn brightly.
Go forward.

Blessings to all.

7TH FEBRUARY

As you pass from one day to another
Remember your origin.
Stop and unite with the Glory of Love
For it is from this point
That the whole of Creation was made.
Therefore at the beginning and end of each day
Give thanks.
Surround yourself with the Light of Love
Then continue.
At the centre point of your day
Stop and remember again.
This time be aware of your surroundings
And join with Love momentarily
Then again continue.
In this way you will develop
Total awareness of the Whole
And stay united with Love.
It is not as easy as it sounds
So be Compassionate and Loving with yourself
And practice with Patience.

Blessings to all.

8TH FEBRUARY

Fear not to go forward.
Do not count each mistake as a total failure
Yet go forward from it
So that you may learn a true lesson
One that will stay with you
Enabling a greater movement along life's highway.
By doing so
You will truly progress
In Body and Soul
For as you are lifted
So shall each step be lighter
And change be easier
Until you have achieved your goal.
Be positive
Even in negative times
For this is how you learn.

Blessings to all.

9TH FEBRUARY

Try as you may
You can never know the outcome of events.
Therefore know this to be True:
"That you can only work with Love
To ensure that you have done your best
For you cannot do any better than that."
How things work out is then up to others.
So look deeply into your Heart of Hearts.
See clearly and then act
Knowing from this place of Truth
All will be as clear as it can be.
Send Love to all.
Be surrounded by Love
Letting the Light go forth
Showing you a pathway
Into a peaceful future.

Blessings to all.

10TH FEBRUARY

Remember
A cup is again useful
Once it is empty.
Therefore allow that which you know
To flow from yourself to others
So that by giving
You may once again receive
Thereby growing
In Wisdom and Understanding
Of the Truth
And the circle held within it.

Blessings to all.

11TH FEBRUARY

Is there a time and place
For the perfect moment or event?
Surely the time and place
Is in the changing Now.
Each second
Each breath
Brings the Gift of Hope.
Therefore look to every second
As a new beginning
And a chance to bring about
That which you desire
Or think that you need.
Just be aware that perhaps
You do not know the whole journey
And because of that
Be open to change.
For events happen
And it is how you cope
That builds and nourishes you.
With this in mind
Walk with Love in your Heart
Sending Love silently to all.
This will illuminate your pathway
And aid others on theirs.

                              Blessings to all.

12TH FEBRUARY

In each Being
There is a still voice
That mirrors the calm waters
Of the Soul.
Come sit silently
By the water's edge.
Look deeply into its stillness
And allow that
Which is reflected
To penetrate
Throughout your Being
For such will bring you
Untold Peace and Joy
And fill you
With the Gift of Love.

Blessings to all.

13TH FEBRUARY

How do you experience yourself
In relation to the world around you?
Are you part of the Whole
Or do you distance and isolate yourself?
If it is the latter
You are missing a vital part of yourself
For by not realizing the unity
You sever a natural connection to the Universe
And all of its Gifts.
It is by living as one Whole
That the Blessings can be found.
These are simple things
From the colours of nature
To the Love of people around you.
By sending Love to all of Creation
You are joined to the universal energy
And you help it move freely
From one life source to another
Thereby uniting with the Whole.

Blessings to all.

As for yourself
Know this to be True:
"That you cannot change anyone
Except by example and Love."
For by showing them a different way
You are giving them a silent choice:
Either to continue as they are
Or to notice Love in all aspects.
Therefore ask yourself
Why should they change?
What is their pathway?
And do you yourself know better?
So walk silently with Love
Being aware of oneself
Doing one's best
And allowing all around you
To discover their own Self
In their own time and way.

       Blessings to all.

15TH FEBRUARY

How long must you wait
Until the realization occurs
That all is made of Love?
For all else has lost true meaning.
Therefore look around you.
Understand Love
Then allow your true potential
To develop – blossom - grow
So you become who you really are:
A child of the Universe
Surrounded by Loving Kindness.
This Knowledge will give you
The strength to go forward.
So gather the Light of Love around you.
Open silently with Love
And allow developments
To open up your pathway before you.

Blessings to all.

16TH FEBRUARY

A peaceful mind
Is one of the hardest virtues
To maintain.
Therefore one needs
To be able to detach oneself
For while the centre is found
In the ego
All will be viewed from self.
In this way
Every event and action
Is labeled
Me and mine.
If one can remove the ego
To an extent
That it only serves
Then a broader vision is the result
And life will be smoother.
What is needed
Is to see
Into the Whole
To widen one's awareness
Knowing that everything passes.

Blessings to all.

17TH FEBRUARY

If you had one wish
What would it be?
Who would it be for?
Surely most would ask for themselves.
Yet with one chance to change the world
How can a wish be singular
Given the unhappiness
And confusion around you?
Know that there is a willingness
For Love to grow in each Heart.
Therefore realizing
That this is the Secret of Life
Ask for Love to enter each person
A Love for all
Sharing Hope
Peace
Compassion
Thus changing the thoughts and actions
Of the entire world.
Start by sending Love yourself
And be aware how this affects you
And your surroundings.

                              Blessings to all.

18TH FEBRUARY

After the rain comes the sunshine.
This in nature
Makes the flowers grow.
Yet it takes both to accomplish this
For without one
The other cannot be productive.
Therefore realize in your own life
That this also holds true
As you are not different
From your surroundings.
Stop and look to your life.
See that in the so called "hard times"
You have come through them and grown
Allowing others to benefit from your experience.
So with Love
And always Love
Go forward
Facing life with a clear Heart
And a true Understanding
Of being in a human form.

                                        Blessings to all.

19TH FEBRUARY

Is there a time better than Now?
Surely Now is the only time there is.
To look back other than to learn
Is to lose the moment.
Likewise to wait until the future comes
Allows precious moments to slip by.
Therefore be bold.
Do what needs to be done in the Now.
By doing so
You will live your life to the full
Facing each day with Hope.
Always look to your Heart for guidance
So that Love is your measure of positive and negative.
By doing this
You will be able to go forward
With the correct attitude
And be a comfort to all
Sharing Light and Love
As you move quietly along your pathway.
Go with Love and Blessings.

Blessings to all.

20TH FEBRUARY

Come all and listen:
Is it not the past
That holds you?
For it is by letting go
And living in the Now
That relief comes.
What was
Is no more.
It is gone.
The future holds all promise.
So be strong.
Give yesterday what is due.
Then from your advantage point of today
Move forward
Into a glorious tomorrow.
Be brave
And live in the Light of Love.

Blessings to all.

21ST FEBRUARY

Gather yourself.
Decide what is positive
Then proceed.
Even in adversity
Hold fast
With a loving Heart.
Do not err from the path
That you have chosen
For what comes
Does so at the right time
In the right way.
Have Faith
Trust
And all will work
For the greater good.

                              Blessing to all.

22ND FEBRUARY

In the quietness
There is a Voice
So quiet
That perfect stillness
Is required to hear it.
One must go inside
So that stillness
Can permeate
The body and mind.
Then and only then
Can the Silent Voice be heard.
So practice with Love
And allow a quietude of both
And learn to listen
To that which is
Your own True Self.

                              Blessings to all.

23RD FEBRUARY

Look and Awareness shall be given.
Ask and you shall truly find
For the true seeker
Shall know the way.
All doors shall be opened
And a pathway extended before you.
Therefore in the mists
Of your troubles and doubts
Stop.
For in doing so
All will be answered
And the earnest Heart
Shall receive Blessings
Beyond earthly thoughts.
For what are you
If not a child of the Universe
And does not a parent
Lead and guide their child
With Love?
So know in your Heart
To follow the Truth
Knowing all else will fall away
And you will be left
In glorious Peace and Light.

                              Blessings to all.

24TH FEBRUARY

In every situation there is Light.
Therefore do not allow yourself
To sink beneath it.
For why are you here
In this time
In this place
If not to learn
The lessons of purpose?
Look around you.
What are the small and large incidents
That make up your life?
Then taking them one by one
Examine and realize each reason.
Then having the realization of them
Move onward
So that each part of you is cleared
Ready to receive Light and Love.

Blessings to all.

25TH FEBRUARY

What is there if not space?
From nothing something develops.
It is this
Which is right for you.
Like a leap in the dark
Your Trust moves outside yourself
Based on the great force
Of Love
Which you are part of.
In this way much will happen
And you will be led along your pathway
Ever experiencing something new
So that you yourself
Will broaden and grow
Until that which is required
Has been reached.
Then in your most useful state
You may be of service.
Trust.
Have Faith
And all will be answered.

                                    Blessings to all.

26TH FEBRUARY

Let light surround you
In your daily existence
So that you reach upward.
Even in the times
When you have doubts
Know a ray of eternal Joy
Penetrates deep within you.
Then in this way
You will always be led onward.
Even in the most difficult moments
Hope will lift your fear
And you will know the Truth
And be able to follow it
Disregarding the smaller self
Going directly to the infinite goal
Which is abounding Peace and Light.

                              Blessings to all.

27TH FEBRUARY

The universe's Gifts are boundless
For those who have eyes to see.
So go slowly through life.
Give yourself time
To recognize the Blessings.
In this way even the smallest event
Becomes a miracle.
The slightest word
Holds encouragement
Which allows you to go forward
Not only to help yourself
But also to assist others
Along their pathway.
For what is life
If help cannot be given?
If we cannot share our
Wisdom with those
Who are ready to receive
And like ourselves
Wish to travel the long journey
Homeward?

                                    Blessings to all.

28TH FEBRUARY

If today is the first day
Of the rest of your life
What will you do with it?
And what of your past
Would you change?
With help
One may start afresh
And learn to equalize
What has been.
By a willing Heart
Filled with Love
It is possible to put right
All the injustices
That have been carried out
So that you are free of the past.
You will be given the strength
To face not only yourself
But others
Putting right any outstanding debts
Until sufficient has been paid back
Allowing you to go freely on your way
Traveling towards the Light
And your correct place in the universe.

Blessings to all.

29TH FEBRUARY   (LEAP YEAR)

Walk in the way of Truth
And Love
For this brings
Heaven on Earth.

Blessings to all.

MARCH

1ST MARCH

Nature moves in its own time.
It has its own rhythm.
So it should be with each of you
Understanding yourselves
And moving within your natural beat.
In this way
You shall know Harmony
Completing that which is necessary
For your own life-span
Allowing that which should be
And letting all else pass by.
Therefore sit.
Become still.
Recognize your Higher Self
And then go with the flow of events
Letting your life slowly unfold before you
Being guided
By Light and Love.

Blessings to all.

2ND MARCH

You know of the words:
  "Look and all shall be given"
For you have the ability to know the Truth.
So look no further than your Heart.
Be happy to know
That what is necessary will develop
If you truly believe.
Therefore go along your way
Firm in your Belief and Love
Knowing that all will be provided
At the right time
In the right way.
For with such Faith
All will be achieved.

Blessings to all.

3RD MARCH

Watch the flowers growing.
See with your Inner eye
Their Life energy.
Feel the gentle strength
That allows them to grow.
Know that even in the most difficult situations
They will continue to strive towards the Light.
Then compare yourself
And your life
So that you too may know
What silent determination is.
Let all else fall away
And proceed
Towards your goal
With Love
For it is there
That you will find true fulfillment
Bathing in the Light of True Being.

Blessings to all.

4TH MARCH

From your Inner Depths
Seek to find that which needs changing.
Once found
Begin a slow and gentle process
To bring about transformation.
At first there will be violent opposition
But slowly
With Loving Kindness to self
There will be change.
Be to yourself as you would be to a dear friend.
Have Patience and Compassion
As you try to hold on
To the old and comfortable
For if you truly wish it to happen
Change will take place.
Then you can be as you should be
Instead of how your whims take you.
Control comes from within
Instead of from your surroundings.
Therefore be still
So you may receive
The strength that is needed
And be guided along your chosen pathway
Until the end of all of your days.

Blessings to all.

5TH MARCH

In the Hearts of humans
There may be turmoil or stillness.
It is how one views Life
That allows one Peace.
Therefore know that you can
Choose happiness or sorrow
For while there is turmoil
Nothing can progress
Only constant movement going nowhere.
But once you have found Peace
If only for a moment
You can take stock
And then allow yourself
To begin the greatest journey of all
One that will lead
To a greater Understanding of many things.
Therefore be still
Surround yourself with the Light of Love.
Know that your Soul purpose
Is to learn and then progress
Towards your True Self
Wherever that leads you
For at the end of your journey
You will be Home.

Blessings to all.

6TH MARCH

From the beginning of time
Humans have wanted.
However wants are not needs.
Therefore look into your Heart
And seek for the reality.
For where is it said that one owns?
Rather it is uttered that one shares.
In this way there are no true belongings.
All that is
Is borrowed
That while you are here
You may have or have not.
Yet further on your journey
All things must be returned.
Even your body is not yours
For all the forever-mores.
Therefore walk quietly with Love
Disturbing as little as possible
For You are what you take with you
Through all of your tomorrows.
So work on self
For this is all that you need.

                              Blessings to all.

7TH MARCH

Come walk together
Being brothers and sisters all.
For is not Love a universal Gift?
Therefore when looking at each other
See yourself.
In this way
You will be quick to praise
And much slower to anger
For there is a universal thread
That passes through humankind
Linking one with another.
It is this thread
That unites all
Bringing Harmony and Peace
To a much-troubled world.
So sit.
Let this golden thread pass beyond self
Thereby bringing Light to all
And joining all in Love.

> Blessings to all.

8TH MARCH

Bring Peace where you can
For is it not said that the Peacemakers
Shall be shown the way for Heaven on earth?
Therefore
Stop.
Before you commit a word into the ether
Think of its vibrations
And then change it if need be.
For it will do harm
Not only in an outward motion
But also in an inward one
So that you would be hurting
Yourself as much as others.
Sit and think of the energy of the spoken word.
Learn to control it
And then move on to the thought behind it.
By changing that to one of Love
Each word will be a Gift to all.

Blessings to all.

9TH MARCH

What is food for the body?
It is not only edible
But also it must be nourishment for the Soul
For one without the other
Will lead to a deficiency.
Therefore to allow positive growth
One should look after both aspects.
Each being given just enough
To promote a healthy balance
So that they are not weighed down
And become heavy
But are given just the right amount
Which will allow what has been accepted
To be absorbed.
In this way nothing is wasted
And all can be used for Good
Thereby allowing
The Balance and Unity
Of Love
To be developed and maintained
As you travel your pathway
Through the forever-mores.

Blessings to all.

1OTH MARCH

Let the Light of Love fill your world
For in this way
You will know that all things
Are as they should be.
The Light itself shall guide and protect you
Turning what appears to be doubt
Into Understanding.
Therefore be still
Not only in the times of solitude
But also during the busy moments of the day.
Dedicate your actions for good.
Seek none of the recognition for self.
In this way what is yours will be given
And will truly be yours to accept.
For should you not all work
Towards the common goal
Of Unity with the One
Which in itself helps to bring the Light down
To fill the Minds and Hearts of all
Thus causing a mirrored reflection
Of the Whole?

Blessings to all.

11TH MARCH

Walk softly
For have you not trod
The same pathway?
Therefore say only that
Which you know to be true.
Pass no judgment
Least you be judged yourself
For do you not all
Have the capacity to improve
If you wish?
So let the first glance be made inward
And the first comment be of self.
In this way
Each step shall be based on Love
And not on the profit from each other
For there is only one judge
And you are just participants
In the great School of Life.

                                    Blessings to all.

12TH MARCH

Time and space are not important.
It is your thought and actions
That take you through such units.
Therefore positive deeds
Filled with Love
Can be used to prolong units
While negative deeds can shorten them.
On this path of Wisdom
There can be found the way
To lengthen one's days
So that each ripple from Self
Only adds to the Greater Harmony.
Check yourself to ensure that you are emitting
Positive energy
One that builds and allows continual upliftment.
In encouraging this
There will be a quiet strength
And it will last to carry you onward.

Blessings to all.

13TH MARCH

Where in all of your days
Do you sing the praise of Creation
And from where do you sing it?
Each thought and word
Should be directly from the Heart.
In this way you will always be heard
For such will be the pure Joy
Behind each uttering
That it will float directly towards the Light.
Speak only of your true feelings
So that you can then surround yourself
With Love.
Seek nothing more.
Know in this there lies the way
Of true Devotion and Understanding
Of your journey.
Be patient with all
Allowing all who seek to find you
And if choosing to
Benefit by doing so.

> Blessings to all.

14TH MARCH

See your surroundings
Know their natural flow
So that no matter how you struggle
What will be
Will happen at the right time
For it to unfold.
Therefore why hasten things with your Heart?
Let them be
And rather slow your Heart down
To the natural pace of life
For if things are to be sustained
They must have their own gentle rhythm.
Therefore look towards nature.
Feel the flow.
Then allow yourself
To move to the greater rhythm
One that has been before time itself
And one that will exist
Even when time has stopped.
Be in no hurry
But attune your breath to the Universe.
Look and see
Then step back
Surrounding yourself with the Light of Love.
Breathe into the Light
Until you become the Light.

Blessings to all.

15TH MARCH

Know that there are many pathways
And many people who walk them.
All are different
Yet all reaching out
Towards the same goal
Which is to become
Part of the glorious Whole.
So work slowly with Love
And know that
You are part of a gentle group of Souls
Whose wish it is to spread the Light
To reach all of humankind.
Trust and work
To shine the Light on all
Who dwell within your radius
For Light pulsates with its own rhythm
And by uniting with it
You will be able to project a greater rhythm.
Work slowly and all will be fulfilled
As you work in Silent Harmony.

Blessings to all.

16TH MARCH

Balance is the key.
Not too much or too little
But just enough to hold the central line.
It is of no use to be too rigid
Or to be too soft.
One must know the Harmony of all things
Which is Love.
Therefore be not quick to judge
But wait and know all events.
Then when each side has been heard
You may choose to hold onto the centre
And try to bring each opposing side
Closer to you.
By doing this you will hold the Balance.
Be silent in your work.
Know the Truth
And bring others closer to the Light
For once they have found themselves
They will have more Understanding of others.
In this way your chosen pathway will unfold
Bringing hope to many
And in doing so
Bringing fulfillment for yourself.

                                    Blessings to all.

17TH MARCH

Each incident is a preparation
That if correctly learnt will lead
To a stronger Soul.
Ask yourself this question: Why?
Then if you still do not understand
Sit quietly.
Surround yourself
With the Light of Love
So that all may be revealed
For the purpose is always there
And it is just for you to fathom.
By doing so
You will be able to develop
Your own Inner Space
And become clearer about your own role
Within the system of giving and receiving.
Know this to be True:
"That the choice is yours.
You can go forward or not
And depending on your decision
So will your learning and growth be measured."

                                        Blessings to all.

18TH MARCH

In each of us is the key
Which may
If used correctly
Open the doorway
To the Universe and beyond.
Therefore sit quietly
And ask for the Light to be given
So that you may be the means
By which Love and Goodness
Can project to all
Allowing those who are searching
And those in need
To find Peace and Harmony
And their own pathway forward.
Read these words again
And act according to your inner-most Heart.

                              Blessings to all.

19TH MARCH

Let the Light surround you
And know that sometimes
A clearing is necessary
For there are occasions when negativity
Is left in the channel.
Therefore sit quietly
And ask for the Blessed Light
So that you may once again
Be used as a pure pathway.
In this way cleansing will take place
And you yourself will feel lighter
Being able to receive and transmit
A stronger radiance of Love.
For do not all instruments of refinement
Need adjusting to maintain perfection?
So why should you be any different?
Are you not the bridge?
"Remember that you work not only for yourself
But also for others."
So you must always strive for perfection
And let it flow to all things.
Thoughts
Words
Deeds
Nothing is separate.
Therefore all must be as pure as it can be.
Work diligently for help is always at hand.

Blessings to all.

20TH MARCH

For such are the transgressions of humankind
That their time on earth
May be filled with pain and discomfort.
Yet if one looks at the whole lifetime
It is rarely that such a time exists.
Rather it is punctuated between pain and pleasure.
Therefore look to the pleasure of both times
And see both as a learning process
Knowing that there comes from
Deep sorrow a greater Understanding
Allowing you to go further along your pathway.
Open yourself with Stillness to Love
And understand each moment
Living your life in the Now
So that your Heart and Mind will expand
With the true meaning of receiving Blessings
Of both sorts with Grace and Humility.

Blessings to all.

21ST MARCH

Do you know where your Gifts come from?
Then to truly receive them
Sit in Stillness.
Open yourself so that you may become truly receptive
And can absorb all that is given.
It is not for you to measure the amount
But rather to be open enough
So that you may receive.
The Light of Love comes from a never-ending source.
It flows down to all.
Therefore by sitting
You may rise to meet this supreme Gift.
By doing so you will be able
To absorb the Light.
So make yourself ready.
Breathe
And with a true Heart filled with Love
You may rise for maximum absorption.
In this way on return
You will be able to understand and offer help
To those who seek you.
All is for the purpose of sharing
And by doing your task to its fullest
You will be spreading the word
And the Light throughout your world.
There can be nothing more.
Go quietly, giving your Gifts in silent Love
Passing along your pathway, and asking nothing
From another Soul in return
For such is the way of true Love and Simplicity.

Blessings to all.

22ND MARCH

Such are the Lessons of Life
For how else shall you learn?
It is your Faith that shall be your strength.
Even when reason fails
And your hopes are dashed
Support will come if you truly believe.
Knowing this will enable you
To face all of Life's lessons
With fortitude and courage.
For they are lessons
Yet the results are beyond
Even your expectations.
So walk slowly
Thereby seeing
All of the beauty
As well as the pain of this world.
Open yourself to the Light of Love
Never forgetting your origin or purpose.
In this way
All will reach its natural conclusion
And you will once again rest
In the Light of Love.

Blessings to all.

23RD MARCH

Look towards your Inner Self.
Do not waste the precious Light
That has been given to you.
Go forward in Truth and the Light
And Trust
For that is where all Truth lies
And all gifts come from.
Be not afraid to step on this pathway
So that you may grow.
There will be errors along the way
But that is how you will learn
And perfect your special Gift.
Open your Heart and Mind.
Ask for help
Letting Love be your guide.

Blessings to all.

24TH MARCH

For it is written
The sun shall never set
On a Heart that is full
Of Love and Understanding.
Therefore grow quiet
So that you can differentiate between
The spoken word and the truthful one.
Look and see.
Confer with what is at hand
To that which is written in your Heart.
Then you will always come back
To the Truth and Light.
Go slowly for it is a long
And sometimes hard road to travel.
But be patient
For one small step
Is all that is required.
Know that each step
Will lead you closer to your goal
That of Truth
Understanding
Peace
And Love.

                              Blessings to all.

25TH MARCH

Fear not to go forward.
Do not count each mistake
As a total failure.
Yet go forward from it
With loving awareness
So that you may learn
A true lesson
One that will stay with you
Enabling a greater movement
Along life's highway.
By doing so you will
Truly progress in Body and Soul
For as you are lifted
So shall each step be lighter
And change be easier
Until you have achieved your life's goal.
Be positive
Even in negative times
For this is how lessons are learnt.

       Blessings to all.

26TH MARCH

If you wish to change your world
Look within.
First start with the smallest seed.
Fill it with Love
Then watch it grow.
It will develop beyond all hope
So that which you dared to dream
Will become a reality.
Let Light and Love
Shine into you
Day by day
Week by week.
Then suddenly you have changed.
The doubts and pain have gone
And all that remains is Love.

Blessings to all.

27TH MARCH

And so it has been
From the beginning of time:
Humans have striven to achieve harmony without
Not realizing that true unfolding
Lies along another pathway.
So now turn inward.
Tread carefully.
Disturb as little as possible.
Let each small quiet step
Be one that brings Wisdom
Of how you live your life.
Then in the fullness of time
All will be revealed
And you will know your own Truth
And with that Wisdom
Comes everything
For as above so below.
Trust
Love
And keep Faith
With yourself.

Blessings to all.

28TH MARCH

What is there
If not Love?
For this small word
Holds the meaning of Life.
The way to perfection
Is through Love.
The way to Love
Is through thought and action
Both joined in Harmony
And being directed
By Love.

Blessings to all.

29TH MARCH

When there is pain and confusion
Try to turn towards your Higher Self.
Look past your small self
And let your being fill
With Love.
Know that you are not alone
And all things have a purpose.
Even if the reason is not clear
It will be.
Let Love shine through the dark clouds.
Let Peace enter your Soul
Until you feel calm and recharged
Knowing that all is moving
Along the right pathway.

Blessings to all.

30TH MARCH

What can be written
In the Hearts of humankind:
Sorrow or Joy?
Yet once you turn
Your face to the Light
The awareness of
True Understanding
Can bring blessed Peace.
In this way
The sorrow and Joy
Are balanced
And life is no longer a mystery.
Awaken your Heart.
Let Love fill you
So much so that it
Grows beyond
The physical boundaries
But can go further
Into the ether
Touching all who come close
Thereby Blessing all.

Blessings to all.

31ST MARCH

Take things slowly.
Do not try to rush.
Walk silently with Love
So that your footsteps
Leave no sound
Except a soft
And gentle breeze.
Then people will know
You have been amongst them
Not by noise
Or disturbance
But by the
Peaceful feeling
That has lingered
Long after you have moved on.

                                    Blessings to all.

APRIL

1ST APRIL

Why continue
 When all seems to be
Going in another direction?
Because you have
Answered the call
Of your own Inner Wisdom.
Therefore nothing can be denied
For it is the Light and Love
That lead you.
It is a golden path
That travels through the grey.
It is Eternity that calls you.
It is the Truth
That one day you will reach.

                        Blessings to all.

2ND APRIL

Even when you are down
Look up.
For it is from there
That hope comes.
Whatever you think
You can rise above basic thoughts.
Let your mind be lifted
Let your Heart soar
And let the eternal Light of Love
Fill your entire Being.
Have Faith.

                                  Blessings to all.

3RD APRIL

There is always hope.
  Hope for yourself
Hope for others.
By others the meaning is all
Even those you would not consider worthy
For who can say with certainty
Or choose with accuracy
Who is worthy?
So let your Hope
Go forward to all.
Let Hope expand and cover all.
Let it grow silently
Until all is included
And filled with it
So that all are able
To move with Love and Light.

                                    Blessings to all.

4TH APRIL

What is a Blessing?
Where does it come from?
Is it from some outer being?
Yes.
But it is also from
The Inner Self.
All can and should give Blessings.
They should flow from you
Like a never-ending stream of Light
Given freely to all
Without question
Thereby allowing yourself
To be fulfilled
By the same source
Allowing a constant circle of Love
To move through and between
All of Creation.

Blessings to all.

5TH APRIL

When you sit
Let Peace surround you
Like a warm blanket
Until it gently enfolds you
With its Love.
For whatever is needed
Love will heal all.
So sit quietly and patiently.
Wait.
Let your mind become calm
Like a pool of clear water.
Watch the ripples slowly
Move to the edge
And disappear.
Then rest
And allow Love
To be all there is
And melt into its open arms.

Blessings to all.

6TH APRIL

Come see for yourself
The difference between
Hope
Trust
And Fear.
Ask yourself
How can you live your life with fear?
For that colours your every thought and action.
With fear you are held back
Stifled.
But with Hope and Trust
You are free to go forward
To move into a place of perfect Balance
So anything that comes to you
Whether it be for better or worse
Can move around you
Yet not disquiet your Being.
So strive for Hope and Trust
And by so doing
Live in the light
Of eternal Love.

                                        Blessings to all.

7TH APRIL

Why frown?
For when you do so
You are visibly holding tension.
What does this mean?
It is that you do not Trust.
By frowning you are showing
That your words hold little or no Faith.
It is different when you smile.
Then the same face shows Trust
But even more important
Love.
So be aware.
When you are going through your day
Check.
Let all tension go.
Breathe the breath of Love.
And allow it to soften you
So that all tension is released
And you are free.

Blessings to all.

8TH APRIL

If you are in need of help
Who do you turn to?
Yes, we all need each other
Yet there are times when
Even our dearest people
Cannot bring the comfort
That is required.
So where do you go?
It is then that you should turn inward
And in doing so
You will find your true answer
For it is only within
That the Truth is found.
The Self knows all
And is the connection
With the Light and Love
And only works for the good of All.

Blessings to all.

9TH APRIL

What can words do?
They have the ability to change worlds.
So let your words come not only
From your lips
But also from your Heart.
Look closely before you speak
For what is once uttered
Cannot be changed.
Words can be like swords
Or like a beacon of Hope and Love
Healing and providing the way
Towards wholeness of Being.
Therefore choose wisely
Always encouraging positive growth
And then quietly watch and wait
For loving roots to grow and blossom.

Blessings to all.

10TH APRIL

Even if you are unsure
Of events in your life
Just look for the good in all things
For you can with ease
Be assured that only your attitude
Will colour them.
See all good things as Gifts
And all else as lessons.
In that way you are
Making your days
As opportunities for moving onwards.
This will enable you to leave
The past behind
And to be held in each moment
Of the Now.

                              Blessings to all.

11TH APRIL

Today there is nothing new under the sun.
So has it always been
Since history has begun.
Yet there are those
Who consider themselves
To be unique and special.
While one's uniqueness is true
The overall scheme of things
Is merely a repartition of Being
So it is important to remember
That one is never alone
Or so special that there is
No accounting for one's thoughts or actions.
Living with this Knowledge
Will bring Peace and Love to the world
Which is the main reason for life on earth.

Blessings to all.

12TH APRIL

There comes a time
When all else shall fade
And what is left
Is pure Light
Pure Being.
So work slowly towards this.
Do not try to rush.
Walk slowly
Then you shall not miss
All of the wonders.
Bring yourself to a place of Stillness
And from there move forward
As you are taken
For you yourself do not realize the way.
Wait and be guided by loving hands.
Trust in the Light
And open your Heart
To Unconditional Love.

Blessings to all.

13TH APRIL

Being still is a way
Of contacting
Your Higher Self.
So always try to find time
Even if it is just for a breath or two
For by forming a time and place
Which is acceptable to you
You are allowing those who Love you
To establish a permanent line of connection.
So make time.
Remember to sit daily
And then rejoice in Unconditional Love.

                                        Blessings to all.

14TH APRIL

Look to the seasons.
See how they change.
Take from nature the Truth
That all is in permanent flux.
Let go of all things
For holding tight
Only makes the natural process harder.
Open your hands and Heart.
Experience yourself as a flowing river
Giving help and nourishment
To all that you encounter.
Then allow them to move on or stay
That being their own choice.
In this way
You become part of the whole of Creation
Guided by an endless stream
Of Loving Kindness.

                                    Blessings to all.

15TH APRIL

Come
Do not waste a moment of time.
Rather work towards Unity
Now.
By putting off each day
You are lengthening the time
Needed to complete your journey.
What is your journey? you ask.
It is your life's goal
The reason that you are here.
To find that
Sit
Wait
And then finding Stillness and Love
Move forward
Holding Love as the flame
For all to see and feel.
So gather yourself and rise
And all shall be given.

                              Blessings to all.

16TH APRIL

As rain waters and feeds
So your thoughts nourish your Being
And your actions nourish
Others around you.
So look to nature.
What is the earth without rain?
What can grow and flourish?
What does it look like?
When you have the answers
To these questions
Think of your place in this world.
Realize what you do and say
Effects not only those around you
But you yourself.
Therefore be aware how important
You are in the cycles of life
And bring only Love to all.

                              Blessings to all.

17TH APRIL

Is there enough Love
To go around?
Yes.
For such a thing
Flows constantly.
Look to the seasons.
As one brings the end
As you see it
Another brings life.
But if you truly look
You see not the end
But a period of rest and gathering.
Then once again it allows
Life to burst forth.
So it is with Love
A continual flow surrounds you.
It is only you that cannot
Be aware at all times
But it is there always with you.
All that is needed
Is to connect
And receive it.

Blessings to all.

18TH APRIL

Come
See for yourself the difference
Sitting makes.
When you give time for Stillness
It reflects in your very Being.
This in turn
Allows your days
To become
Clearer and more peaceful.
So by giving time
You will reap the untold benefits.
Therefore allot an amount for yourself
And give this joyfully
Not asking or expecting
But allowing what is right
To unfold within and before you.
By listening with your Heart
You will hear the sound
Of Unconditional Love.

Blessings to all.

Come
Sit.
Be Still.
It is not only in the doing
That great things happen.
First there must be Stillness
For the idea to enter
Then movement is necessary.
So learn to be quiet
Peaceful
And open to the positive.
Then and only then
Can the change begin to unfold.
It may come quickly
Or take time.
But be assured
That change for good will happen
In the right way
At the right time.
All happens with Love.

Blessings to all.

20TH APRIL

Invest in Life.
Look around you.
What do you see?
Let only the positive stay with you
For all passes.
Even the sad times do not stay.
So enjoy that which
You have been given.
Know that even that too will pass.
This will allow you
To go forward
To meet your future
With Love
Giving you the opportunity
To have many new beginnings.
So be thankful for all.
Learn to trust
And open yourself
To Life's Gifts.

Blessings to all.

21ST APRIL

In the middle of your day
Stop.
Look back.
Realize your thoughts
Words and deeds.
Follow them to this point
And ask yourself
Could I improve the day?
By doing this you will be able
To change what is necessary
Or to continue with your day.
Either way you will have enhanced
Yourself and those around you
Giving all the opportunity
To act
With Love
And Compassion.
This will allow the world
To turn with Love.

Blessings to all.

22ND APRIL

From shining Light comes Hope.
Yet without darkness
How can you know Light?
So it must be with life
For with only Light
There would be no Understanding
Of the goodness
That each person is capable of.
This is the Truth.
It may be hard to comprehend
But the simple Truth always is.
So look to each day
With a loving Heart
And as a chance
For positive growth
Rejoicing in the good times
And Understanding
Life's lessons.

Blessings to all.

23RD APRIL

Love can and will wait.
For whatever reason there is
Love will keep faith.
This means that Love has endless patience.
While you go about your days
Thinking of the most important things to do
Love silently holds you.
Then when the realization comes
That all but Love passes
Love shall be there
Only a breath away
Waiting to help to bring Peace
And an awareness of Truth
Which in turn will help you
In your daily life.
Love is always at hand.
Just be still and it is with you.

Blessings to all.

24TH APRIL

So that there can be no mistake:
It is your thoughts
Words and deeds
That will eventually return to you.
Therefore review your daily life.
By doing so
You will be able to correct any misdeeds
That have slipped by
For what is given out
Even unknowingly
Will be noted
And in due course return
Only then it will be a harder lesson to learn.
Corrections can easily be made
By sending out Blessings
And Love to all
And if necessary asking forgiveness.

Blessings to all.

25TH APRIL

Each day there is the possibility
To grow a little closer
To your True Self.
By this it is meant
To learn how to find Inner Stillness
And listen to the Silence within
For it is in the Silence
That all can be found.
So remember
And keep coming back
To your centre.
Look inwards
Past old habits
Thoughts and feelings
And move to a place where
All is calm.
Even if it takes time
You will discover it.
And from there
You will proceed
To grow towards
Awareness of Being.
So travel slowly with Love.

Blessings to all.

26TH APRIL

Look no further than yourself
For in you is all that there is.
You are made up
Of all of the elements of Life:
The minerals of earth
The emotions of the seas
The changes of the weather.
Why is this?
It is because
All is One.
There is no separation.
What you see around you
Is what you Are.
So walk gently
Knowing that you
Are one part
Of the whole of Creation.
Walk with Love and Compassion.

Blessings to all.

27TH APRIL

What are you looking for?
What do you seek?
Is it external glory
Or is Peace of mind your goal?
Wishes for the former
Will only be passing
While the latter brings
Eternal comfort.
So consider the question
Then relate it to your life.
Look deep into your Heart
And realize what it is
Driving you onward.
If need be
Change with Love
All that is needed
To provide you with Joy
Then proceed along your pathway
To the Light.

Blessings to all.

28TH APRIL

Is it justice that holds you
Or is it mercy?
Do you not know yet
That both must work together?
There can be no leaning
Towards one or the other.
Both must hold equal sway
For if you move too far
In one direction
You cannot understand
The true meaning of events.
So in all things
Strive to be balanced
Allowing clarity of Mind and Heart.
In this way
All shall be clear
And all shall work as it should
Leaving you with a peaceful
Loving Heart.

Blessings to all.

29TH APRIL

Ask yourself
If you should be judged
What would be said?
Is it that you tried
Even though you did not always succeed
Or that you walked away
Leaving others to help?
Look deeply into your self.
Answer truly
Then prepare to try to make amends
If necessary.
Not by going out to do great deeds
But by helping in your own realm.
By sending Love
You can accomplish a great deal
So send Love to the world
And know that you are helping all.

Blessings to all.

30TH APRIL

If it is beauty that you seek
Look no further than yourself.
For within you is all that is
Good
Kind and Loving.
This is found by sitting still
And in the Silence that follows
You will find everything
That you consider to be an outer value.
The human being has all
That is required for a peaceful existence
One that is in harmony
With the flow of nature.
So find the time
And all will be revealed.
Allowing you to find your True Self
And wonder in your own beauty.

Blessings to all.

31ST APRIL

There is always time to change.
If you truly wish to
You will be able to find
The Stillness within.
This will allow
Positive change to develop.
So look to the future
Leaving the past behind
And concentrate
On what matters Now.
By doing this you will be able
To move into a place
Of Peace and Acceptance
Allowing you to settle
Into the realms
Of Unconditional Love
For yourself and others.

                                    Blessings to all.

MAY

1ST MAY

So shall it be
As it always was.
People will follow their Hearts.
Even if they do not trust
There comes a point when
Nothing else will do.
It is then and only then
That they shall find
True Peace and Happiness
For what is life
If it is not lived for purpose?
It may take time
But slowly
The Heart will speak
And nothing will stand in its way
For Love will always
Find its own way
Of Being.

                              Blessings to all.

2ND MAY

"Let there be Light!"
What is the meaning of these words?
Do they just mean external light
Or do they have a deeper meaning?
Yes to both.
For you need your external light
So that you can make your way in this world
Helping you to choose correctly.
But there is also a stronger Light.
This one is within you.
It Lights your Inner Being
And can bring you to a place
Of Peace and Beauty
Which will radiate outwards.
It is this Light that you should nourish
Allowing each one of you to join
In loving Compassion
Thus making the Whole.

Blessings to all.

3RD MAY

What did you come here for?
If it is not to radiate Love
Then why?
Surely the only reason can be
To know how to Love
For by doing so you can save
Not only yourselves but others.
Imagine a world full of Love
Where all is peaceful
And full of Compassion.
Do not say no
But start with yourself
Then as you live
You will understand the difference
Such an existence can make.
Firstly it must come from you
Then others will begin to understand and follow.
So walk slowly and with Love
And realize your true purpose.

Blessings to all.

4TH MAY

Love
There is no other word.
All words
Thus all actions
Emanate from Love.
It is the keystone
Of existence.
How else would the world survive
If not for Love?
Love brings with it
Harmony and Grace.
It allows Compassion
To flow through Creation
Giving each individual
The chance to know their place
Within the structure
Of that which lives.
To walk with Love
Brings Peace.
To walk without
Brings Chaos.
Therefore choose Love
Thereby helping the Universe
To flow as it should.

Blessings to all.

5TH MAY

How would you have your world?
"Perfect."
What does this mean?
It would mean different things
To all people
So even if your idea of perfection
Could be reached
There would still be conflict
Which is why the world
Needs to understand
Love and Compassion.
It is your job
As free-thinking humans
To find a way of creating
Peace and Harmony.
By doing so
You are joining in the act of Creation itself
Thereby bringing Love into Being.

                                          Blessings to all.

6TH MAY

Tread softly
For even by doing so
You will leave a footprint.
This is necessary
For those who come after you
Allowing them to follow
In the way that you have shown.
Therefore look to yourself
Knowing that how you live your life
Will send echoes around the world
Thus creating a space that can
Either attract or repel the Light.
As it is Light that allows Love to flourish
Work only in the realization
That what you do
Say and think
Should be worthy of Love.

Blessings to all.

7TH MAY

It is good to wonder
And ask questions
For if you do not
You will accept many untruths.
What is correct for others
May not be for you.
So listen
Hear and then contemplate.
Decide what is your Truth.
This means being open to others
Yet following your own pathway.
For at the end of your days
Only your voice will be heard
And you will have to justify
Your own Being.
Work gently
And always with Love.

Blessings to all.

8TH MAY

What is morning?
It is a time for beginnings
And for renewal.
So let go of yesterday's events
Facing the new day
With Hope and Love
For by holding on to the past
You bring with you
All of your old habits.
Some may be good
While others are a hindrance.
By allowing yourself to be free
You can experience life
As a new and exciting adventure.
Should some situations arise
You have within you
All that is required
To deal with events
As they should be.
This is with Compassion and Love
For how else is life to be lived?

Blessings to all.

9TH MAY

If what you seek
Does not materialize
Do not worry or fret.
Just be still
And understand
That at this point in your life
What you thought was right for you
Is not.
Your ultimate goal may be true
But the time is not yet here.
So wait.
Then as time and events unfold
There will be a realization
Of what will and should be.
Learn to accept with Love
And all shall prove to be correct.

Blessings to all.

10TH MAY

Each day has its own rhythm.
It is for you to understand
And flow with it.
By doing so you will
Allow whatever occurs
To move towards
Then away from you.
By holding on to no-thing
You become the watcher of all.
This then is the secret of Life
So simple
Yet hard to follow.
Be open to what comes.
Do your best.
Then let go.
Hold no-thing
Positive or negative
For all must change
And all move with Love.

                              Blessings to all.

11TH MAY

In everyone there is a Light.
For some it shines brightly
Others have a softer flame
Yet they know that it is there.
And then there are those who
Do not realize that within themselves
There is all that is required.
It is to these people
As well as others
That Light and Love should be sent.
Sending Love to all
Is the primary reason
For Being.
So I say unto you
Do not choose
But rather
Radiate Love to all.
Do this silently.
Give Blessings.
Smile
And Light and Love
Shall spread
Even in these times
When it is most needed.

Blessings to all.

12TH MAY

What is your hurry?
Stop.
Wait.
Listen to your Heart
For it is only in the quiet space
Of your Inner Being
That your True Self
Can be heard.
While the world goes on around you
In a rush and great noise
You yourself have the key
To Peace and Stability.
So pause.
Breathe gently.
Then with greater Understanding
Quietly move on.
Thereby walking in the pathway
Of Love and Compassion
You will have
True Understanding of life.

                              Blessings to all.

13TH MAY

Into each life
Some tears must fall.
These words are true
For most people
While some others find
That they have been deluged.
So how can they continue?
It is by knowing
That even the heaviest shower
Will move on
Leaving behind the opportunity
For fresh growth.
Thus having been watered
It nourishes the events of Life
Thereby giving all that is required
To move to a better place
With greater Understanding of Self
And of others.
With this awareness
Handle all with Love.

                                    Blessings to all.

14TH MAY

Even if you do not think so
You are special.
For in each of you is a Light.
This Light is always there
Continually shining.
It is for you to remember this
And in troubled times
Turn inward to connect with it.
For by doing so
You will find Peace
Strength
And Love
Which will be of help to you.
Therefore realize
To whom this Light is connected
And learn to trust that it holds
All of the help
And Love
That you require.

Blessings to all.

15TH MAY

Time passes.
This you can be certain of.
So whatever happens in your life
That you consider
Positive or negative
It all will travel from you.
Then what is the point
Of trying to hold on to events?
Rather learn from them
For by treating all as lessons
You can allow your life
To be one of Peace
Letting go of all
And taking with you
A greater Understanding of Self.
All is for a loving growth
A movement toward
Understanding and Wisdom
And with practice
Love will flow to and from you.

Blessings to all.

16TH MAY

In all of the noise and bustle around you
Stop.
Where are you going?
Are you moving into a place
Of Peace and Happiness?
Or is the move
Making no difference whatsoever?
Then finding the answer to your question
Decide what would bring such a move
For move you must.
It is not possible to stand still.
You must either move forward
Or you will miss
Your Life's opportunity.
So think.
Then take the appropriate choice
Allowing Love to be your deciding factor.
Freedom and Joy will follow
And all shall be as it should.

Blessings to all.

17TH MAY

Should there be a reason
For a good life?
Is it not proper that each
Should be happy?
Yet what is happiness?
And how does it translate
Into people's lives?
It is for each of you
To answer that question
For happiness and contentment
Must start and finish within Self.
Therefore take a long look
Into your Heart of Hearts
And it will tell you
Everything that you ask
Allowing you to move from
A place of Truth and Love.

Blessings to all.

18TH MAY

After looking deep within
What did you find?
Is it what you expected
Or are you surprised?
Did you think that you
Would be perfect?
Yet know that all in human form
Are here to learn.
This can only take place by lessons.
So it is through dealing with life
That your Spirit can grow.
Therefore take each situation
As a learning opportunity.
Be thankful
And treat each experience
With Truth and Love
Thereby opening up your Inner Being
To the Light.

                                    Blessings to all.

19TH MAY

In each of you
There is a Light.
It is always burning
Hidden in the deepest part of your Being.
When you are lost or confused
It is that Light
That helps to lift you up
Letting you carry on
And move forward.
Sometimes you remember it
And allow it to lift you
To a Higher Awareness.
On other occasions
It will carry you onward
Without your conscious consent.
But it is always there
To help you
Keep your connection
To Love and Hope.

                                    Blessings to all.

20TH MAY

It is only in troubled times
That one seeks help
Where solace can be found.
While happiness prevails
You do not look for its source
But accept without question
Or indeed give thanks.
So which is more important to you?
You would probably say
The happy times.
But unless they are filled with awareness
We would say the troubled times.
For it is then and only then
That you strive for answers
To the deeper questions
That lead to the Truth.
These questions can
And do change your awareness
And bring you a greater Understanding
Of Love and Truth.

Blessings to all.

21ST MAY

Know this to be True:
That Light and Love are yours.
There is no barrier that exists
Except the one in your mind.
Therefore when using the word Freedom
Firstly relate it to yourself.
Realize that you are free to choose:
Either to live in fear and be caged
Or to live in Light and be free.
Is there a choice?
Let Light and its Gift of Love flow freely
Then let your Mind and Body react.
Notice how you soften mentally and physically.
Then having chosen
Follow that pathway.
Even if you forget and stumble
Stand and regain awareness
Then move onward.
You have all of the time that you need.
Take it.
Use it well.
Let it always bring you back to Light and Love
And follow with the whole of your Being
Until the end of your days.

Blessings to all.

22ND MAY

What is Space?
People today have lost the true meaning.
They look outside themselves
Asking others where to find it.
Yet the only way to experience
True Space and Peace
Is to search inwardly
Looking to oneself for all of the answers
For who else knows you better?
See the darkness and the Light
And then allow the Light to flow through
Covering and filling until all is Light.
By continual practice the Light will expand
Until radiant Light and Love shine from you
And you will live in the glorious Space
Of your True Self.

                                        Blessings to all.

23RD MAY

Let your Heart be filled with Love
So that Light may shine from you.
This will be your Gift to all
Allowing you the wonderful ability
To serve humankind.
Even in your times of doubt
Know for certain that you are not alone
So that self-doubt can vanish
Leaving only the Joy
Of recognition of your purpose.
For what else is there
But to bring Hope and Peace
To all?
So look firstly to Self
Then radiate to others
Thus spreading Love
To each and everyone you meet.

Blessings to all.

24TH MAY

If you had one wish
What would it be?
Is it for self?
Or family?
Or yet further
Would it be for all of humanity?
But first you must ask
Is wishing a help or hindrance?
From your viewpoint
You must first ponder
What do you know?
Do you understand that wishing
Might turn out to be negative?
So before you wish
Ask only that events are for the good of all.
That is sufficient.
For you cannot and do not
Have the greater Understanding.
Therefore sit and send Love to all.
In this way your wish
Will accomplish the greatest good
You could ever do.

Blessings to all.

25TH MAY

There are different ways of loving.
These ways all include
Allowing the loved one space
Giving understanding to their needs
And seeing them as individuals.
All of these lead to a healthy relationship
One that can be based on trust and true Love.
Yet there is another way
Still called Love
Yet removed
From the true meaning of the word.
This way has its roots in possession
Never allowing growth or expression
Holding tightly to the person and wishing to mould
 them.
This is not Love for another
But rather fear within one's self.
It is a failing of confidence
That makes the person only secure
When all is as they wish
Wanting their little world to stretch to all.
So look carefully to yourself.
Give Respect
Compassion and Love
In its true meaning
Thereby adding to the Light of the world.

 Blessings to all.

26TH MAY

It is essential to open your Heart
To receive Love
For how else will you be able
To cope with the arrows of Life?
Look around you
And bring into your centre
The Joy of colour and Being
For what you see radiating
Around you is only a different manifestation of Self.
Therefore acknowledge this to be True
And accept with Grace these Gifts.
Each person knows hard times
Yet by turning to nature
One sees and understands much.
Let the colour of green calm you
The yellows give a gentle warmth
The pinks tenderness
The reds energy.
While the blues heal
Mauve will bring you back to Spirit.
Use these gifts wisely.
And in the presence of them
Ask that you may absorb their rays of Love.
Then give thanks for their help
Returning their Love with a Blessing.

Blessings to all.

27TH MAY

Let others move around you
But you yourself stay still
Only moving a little at a time
So that all may see
How Stillness plays an important role in life.
For those who would spin
Can only have a misty view
Missing most of the detail and true meaning
While those who know Stillness
Can absorb the Whole
And then take action
 With proper Understanding
Of the entire situation.
Therefore look no further than Self
And see all else as distraction.
For when Self is balanced and in Harmony
So too will be your world.
Make this your aim
Devoting your time to allow this to develop
For all else is naught
And holds no bearing
In the way to find the Light of Love.

Blessings to all.

28TH MAY

Think of your attitude.
Ask yourself how do you fare
With those around you?
Do you have favorites?
And do you show it?
Or can you change this fact
And treat all as equal in your interest?
For not only those who help are sent to you
But also those who you call a hindrance.
Therefore how do you look at all?
Each should be made to feel as brother and sister
And not labeled better or worse
For if allowed all help to bring you
Closer to the Light.
Knowing this to be true
Look at each person with your genuine attention
So that you may truly see their origins.
Let this be your Gift to them.
Some will need help
Others a silent prayer
But all need the Blessing of Love.
Think well on this.

Blessings to all.

29TH MAY

Have belief in yourself.
Do not try to be another
For each one of you
Is special in your own way
And to try to copy
Would be to lose
One's identity and uniqueness.
Therefore look to yourself
And offer that which you are
Thereby giving that which is important.
For what greater Gift can there be
If not yourself?
Even if you give a smile
A kind word
A thought
A Blessing
Know that these are special and important
As they allow the Light of Love
To shine and spread through the world.
So remember these words and give freely of Love
Allowing a circle to form around all
Whom you come into contact with
And then beyond them
To the whole of Creation.

Blessings to all.

30TH MAY

What is your wish
    For the children of this earth?
Do you hold fear
Giving only negative thoughts?
Or can you open your Heart
And share your Love of life?
Surely you should send Love
For by doing so
Your Heart will open further
And the benefits will be felt
By yourself as well as others.
So hold fast to your Belief
That Love truly conquers all.
In this way
You can be firm in the Knowledge
That you have played your part
In the future of your race
And have added to the Light
Which is needed to lift humankind.
So stop.
Re-remember your purpose
And then with great Joy and Love
Share your thoughts freely
Being aware of your surroundings
Allowing Peace and Joy to flow to all.

                              Blessings to all.

31ST MAY

As today closes
So too does another period of your time.
This time is never to be repeated
In your life-span.
Therefore look back
And see what has been achieved
And what has been missed.
For your time passes quickly
And from day to day you forget and lose
What has taken place.
In this way many lessons have been lost.
So take time to remember
To understand your own actions
And interactions with others.
By doing so
You will understand much
Not only of people around you but also of yourself.
This in turn will lead to
A clearing and moulding of self
Allowing you to fulfill your goal in this forevermore
Which is to bring Love and Light.

Blessings to all.

JUNE

1ST JUNE

What will you put in this measure of time?
For the choice is truly yours.
You may use it to expand
Or to stay the same
Or even to go backwards.
Whichever you choose
Know that only you have done so.
Do not blame or praise any outside influence
For this would not be true.
At this stage of your life
You must know that you make your own decisions
And therefore other people
Have little or no sway over you and your deepest beliefs.
Therefore any change comes from your Self or self.
It is for you to allow which one comes forward.
Be patient in your dealings with self
For as such
You are your only life's long companion.
For although there are others
You may not recall them.
Therefore place in this time
The best of what you have been.
In this way you will be sure to move closer to your goal
And have a stronger connection
To the Light of Love.

Blessings to all.

2ND JUNE

"Every thing has its place
And there is a place for everything."
Such is the way of life.
Therefore what happens is of vital importance
To the individual.
For once you believe
There is no such thing as chance or an accident
You can relate that to each situation
Knowing if you have given your best
Then what transpires is meant.
For what more can you do?
You can accept this or not.
If you do then your life will run smoothly
So that you can turn your disappointment
Should there be any
Into positive action.
That will lead you to where you should be.
In this way you will always
Be in the Light of Love
Working for the good of all.

Blessings to all.

3RD JUNE

Just as the time around you changes
So too does the climate.
Yet you yourself have the strength of purpose
To stay with the same Belief
To hold onto the Truth.
Even in troubled times
When all else is without conviction
You can hold fast to the Understanding and Wisdom
That have been given to you
For in that is your strength
And the ability to go forward.
How else will you be able to do your work
If not by steadfastness and honesty?
These being the steps along the way.
Therefore sit and know
That all has been given
With Light and Love
And all will be well.

Blessings to all.

4TH JUNE

Words are often uttered needlessly
And said in haste
Without proper awareness of their meaning
Or the consequences of having said them.
This in turn brings unhappiness
To all people involved.
Therefore think hard before
Freeing such vibrations on the ether
For only kind and gentle words should be uttered
Ones that bring positive creativity and Love
To this world and all of its inhabitants.
Even in negative situations
Look always for the shortest way
Of ending the dispute
Thus allowing others to understand fully
And if necessary to change their views.
But if change cannot be reached
Carry on in your own way
With as little disturbance as possible
To yourself and your version of the Truth
Letting go of all hostile thought
Knowing each is on their own pathway
And is responsible for themselves alone.

Blessings to all.

5TH JUNE

As the hands of time turn
Golden moments pass by.
These times can never again
Be replaced or recaptured
Therefore put in them
That which you would wish to remember
For what is a reality today
Is but a memory tomorrow.
How then would you look back?
To happy times
Or to ones filled with sadness?
Place in them what you will.
Hold on to the negative or positive.
It is right for you and you alone to decide
And if you choose the Light
Work towards that end:
Light in radiance - meaning colour
Light in being   -   meaning weight of thought
So that Heart and Mind may be lifted
And filled with Love
Taking you forward to your tomorrows.

Blessings to all.

6TH JUNE

Hold on to no thing.
Let past events go.
This will allow you to be free
To start each day
As a new beginning
Thereby opening yourself
To the possibility of great happiness.
Why hold on to the past?
Whether happy or sad
It has gone.
Acknowledging this will bring Peace of mind
Which in turn will help you
To decide your future.
So past has gone
Future awaits you.
Only Now can bring the changes
That you seek.
So live in the Now
And by living with Love
Tomorrow will come
With the Gift of Hope.

Blessings to all.

7TH JUNE

Look around you.
At each season
There are clues
At every moment there is guidance.
Nature can allow you
A greater Understanding of Life.
For is not all circles?
Yet within each circle
The beginning is never the same
For you learn and start again
With greater Knowledge and Wisdom
Thus allowing you the opportunity
To move forward in a newer
State of Being.
So stop.
Wait.
Gather that which has been given
And with gratitude and Love
Move slowly forward.

Blessings to all.

8TH JUNE

What comes - goes.
What happens - passes.
Who you are – changes.
Just one thing remains constant:
"That which you truly are
Your Self."
It is the only part of you and your life
That stays the same.
So let all else come to you
Then let it go.
Understand that you can hold on to no thing.
By allowing this to be known
Your life will become smoother
And you can hold your still centre
Which is the home of Love
And Compassion for all.

Blessings to all.

9TH JUNE

If there has to be a difference
Who will make it?
Do you wait for someone else
To make the first move
Or is it for you to show the way?
And what difference
And how to show it?
It is for Self to lead.
To be an example of Stillness
So that others will want to follow
Not by force or strength
But by Love and Compassion for all.
Others may not know why
But they will be pleased
To stay near you
For you will radiate
A silent Peace and Love
And from that all changes
Will take place.

Blessings to all.

10TH JUNE

So it shall be
That each must take responsibility
For what happens in their life.
It is too easy to blame others
To pass on all ownership of self.
Yet there comes a time
That one must stand up
And face that which has been created.
It is only then
That true development takes place
Thus allowing self to grow.
Therefore look no further than your own Being
If improvement is required.
Then with Truth and Love
Redress that which is needed
And in doing so
Move forward to the Light.

                                    Blessings to all.

11TH JUNE

Wishing in desperation
Is not the way
For when you are desperate
There is a tightness
That closes oneself
From the centre.
Therefore understand
That there is a difference
Between longing
And being desperate.
Once you grasp this meaning
You are at once
Open to the possibilities
That will occur.
So have Trust.
Allow yourself
To be in a place of Love
And then wait for events to unfold
As they should.

Blessings to all.

12TH JUNE

To have a connection
You must firstly obtain Stillness
For in great movement
All is lost.
When speeding
One loses the ability
To see clearly
Thereby not recognizing
What is around you.
So stop.
Breathe.
Wait.
Be patient with yourself
And in the Stillness that follows
You will be free to understand
That all is Love
And in that Love
Is the possibility of all.
This Understanding will encourage
Comfort and support you
Through the coming years
Allowing you Grace and Serenity.

Blessings to all.

13TH JUNE

Your new beginning is Now.
Not sometime in the future
But in this very moment
You have the ability to start anew.
Should there be something
That you wish to change in yourself
Each moment can bring the opportunity
To move towards
That which you wish to be.
So start slowly
By first filling yourself with Love.
Then with Compassion
Allow the opening to take place
Letting go the old
And welcoming the new.

Blessings to all.

14TH JUNE

If there is a difference
Between what you have
And what you hoped for
Stop.
Look around you
At the many Blessings that you have
For at each moment
You are surrounded with Love:
The Love of nature
Giving forth of itself.
The Love of others
Known and unknown to you
And your ability to return your Love
Thus making an endless circle
Of Love
Compassion
And Hope.

                                        Blessings to all.

15TH JUNE

Just as the sun shines
So the rays of goodness
Radiate to all.
So let your awareness open
Reaching outward and upward to the Light.
Look no further than Self
For when you realize this Truth:
"That you have
All you will ever need
Within you"
You will be able to sit
And become Still.
Allowing your connection
To the loving rays
Which will open your True Being
And fill you with Love.

                                    Blessings to all.

16TH JUNE

From within you
Comes a flame
Which burns brightly.
This flame is eternal
And moves with you
Throughout your existence.
By understanding this
You will realize that you
Are always connected
To Unconditional Love.
This Love is for you
And also for others.
Just as a river flows
So too does your ability
To give and receive Love
For Love is never ending.
It is free of barriers
And is the Greatest Gift of all.
So let it flow freely
And be Blessed.

Blessings to all.

17TH JUNE

Words spoken
Cannot be taken back
For they mark out
And take space in the ether.
By taking space
They send vibrations outward.
These are felt
By all who are sensitive
For they create an energy field
Of their own
Which will remain long after
They are spoken.
Therefore
Think.
Wait.
And in the appropriate way and time
Utter your words
Allowing them
To bring Comfort and Help.
Do so with Loving Kindness.

Blessings to all.

18TH JUNE

Take a look at your life.
See all of your Blessings.
Count them
And you will realize
That there are so many.
Then give thanks.
Understand that you are cared for
Loved and cherished
For even in troubled times
Love still flows to you
And around you
Giving you strength
To move forward.
So share that Love
Either with words or a silent thought
And what you receive will multiply
As you give Love to others.

Blessings to all.

19TH JUNE

Is there some deep wish
That has not been fulfilled?
Some longing that has not been answered?
If you say yes
Then ask yourself why.
Are you stopping this from happening?
Or is it just a dream
That you only wish to hold in your Heart?
For if the time is not right
Then it is better to realize
That it is best left alone
And proceed to live your life
In the present
Appreciating with Love
And giving thanks
For all of the things
That are yours
To treasure in the Now.

Blessings to all.

20TH JUNE

Why rush?
Do you realize
That time has it own rhythm?
It will pass
Regardless of what you do.
So take measure.
Decide what it is that needs to be done.
Then by moving gently
All can be achieved.
Be grateful
And send Love
So that your deeds
May become a Blessing to all.
In this way
By giving and receiving
The Gift of Love
You shall enjoy your labour.

Blessings to all.

21ST JUNE

Each day is a new opportunity
To bring into your world
That which you wish to be there.
So start as you mean to go on.
Even if you have been below
Your expectations yesterday
Today is a chance to change.
So on awakening
Smile.
Think only of the Glory of the day
Then let Love flow through you
Allowing yourself
To be surrounded with Love
Imagining it reaching everyone
That you come into contact with
And then move gently
Through your day.

Blessings to all.

22ND JUNE

Time passes.
Yet within each of you
Is an element of Stillness.
It is from there
That all movement emanates.
So look inward.
Contact that space
Then let it radiate outward
And lead you into your daily actions.
With this in mind
Your encounters
Will have a new meaning
And you will become aware
Of your purpose
In this world
Which is simply to
Radiate Love.
No more.
No less.
For this is the Greatest Gift of all.

                                    Blessings to all.

23RD JUNE

Even if you think that
You are not doing
What is right for you
By stopping and looking around
You will realize
That you
Are where you should be
Doing what is needed
At this time.
Therefore trust.
Perform your tasks
With Love and Patience
And all will be given
At the right time
In the right way
For all to benefit.

Blessings to all.

24TH JUNE

Think of Stillness
As a time for Inner growth.
Do not despair
Because you cannot
Complete your everyday routine
For perhaps you need to take stock
To be able to shed
The unwanted and the unnecessary
So that only what is needed
Will come through.
Therefore at such times
Rest.
Regroup yourself.
Disregard what has become an old habit.
Think more of your Inner Self
And of Loving Kindness.
Let go of external influences.
Then at the right time
All will come into fruition
And all that will take place
Will have its own purpose.

Blessings to all.

25TH JUNE

Always listen to your Inner Heart
For it is that Self
That you have to live with.
Know that what lies before and after
Is of little consequence.
It is that voice of calm reason
That central feeling
That picture
That has to be answered.
If you start by a feeling of discomfort
Then events will only travel
Further along that road.
But if you know
That you have done your best
Then you can stand with a pure Heart
And proceed with Love
Along your pathway.

Blessings to all.

26TH JUNE

Your time on earth may sometimes be filled
With tension and anxiety.
This causes you to close your self.
However if you work with Love
Then all things take on a different hue.
You can go forward each day
Filled with the Knowledge and Wisdom
That being the best of yourself can give.
By giving
People do not take
And you yourself are free to experience
Strength and security
Allowing you to have
A greater capacity.
Walk softly
So that you will be ready to act in the name
Of True Love.

                                        Blessings to all.

27TH JUNE

Let life flow naturally
So that you learn to follow
The stream.
Notice how a river
Will make its way
Sometimes singing and laughing
Sometimes silently
Yet always moving towards its goal.
Even when obstacles block its path
It simply moves around them
Thereby creating as little fuss as possible.
Be like the water:
Moving towards the Light
With as little fuss as will allow
For in this way you will become
A continual source of help to others
Having an endless amount
Of Love to share.

                                    Blessings to all.

28TH JUNE

If what you seek is within you
Why do you look outside?
Do you not know
That all else
Is a false reflection
That the Truth only begins
When you firstly learn
To enter into your deeper Self
And by cleansing and Understanding
Will you begin your journey.
You must be able to say
That you know yourself
From your very roots
How everything that you
Say and do is linked
The positive and the negative.
In this way
You will have a firm base to travel from.
Allow this Knowledge
To let you move along your pathway
With Compassion and Love
For yourself and others.

Blessings to all.

29TH JUNE

Give generously
For this is the only way
To truly share.
When others require your time
Ask why?
Then if it is for the good
Allow your attention to be turned towards them.
Take special care
To make sure that they know
That they hold your interest
And that you will devote yourself
To their requirements.
Then having achieved your best
Pass onward
For you must not allow yourself
To be used as a crutch.
For the purpose of sharing
Is to enable each person to stand
On their own merit
So that they know their own worth.
Therefore be humble
Knowing that all moves towards the Light
With Love.

Blessings to all.

30TH JUNE

What do you seek
If not the Truth?
For with such Knowledge comes Wisdom.
This is not the thoughts of others
But rather a deeper perception of personal matters.
Therefore look more closely at yourself
At your reactions to others.
In this comes the recognition of your smaller self
And with Understanding comes
The ability to change.
Do not expect quick results
Rather go slowly
And take much encouragement
In small steps.
For what is small in appearance
Is in fact a great step
In true Understanding.
Walk along your own pathway
So that the Light of Love
Illuminates your way.

Blessings to all.

JULY

1ST JULY

Take Heart
For even if you forget
Know there is a thread
A Light
That runs through constantly.
This beam is holding all together.
It is at the very centre
Of your being
Lighting your way
Bringing you safely back
To where you should be
Until you are ready to continue
Upon your journey.
So walk with this Knowledge:
That you are guided and protected
With Love
That each step is counted
Until you reach your goal.

Blessings to all.

2ND JULY

Look around you.
Nature has its own way
Of renewing and replenishing itself.
Therefore take note:
By gently following
The rhythm and flow
You too can wait
Until the right time
To bring about the positive changes
That you desire.
Be patient
For all will happen
When it should
Not a second before or after.
So perform your tasks
With Love
Letting Love flow to all
Knowing all is for the good.

Blessings to all.

3RD JULY

How do you live
In this day and age?
You should surround yourself
With Light and Love
For by doing so
You will be able to move
With comfort and ease.
This in turn
Will send
Rays of Love
Around and from you
To all of Creation
Allowing positive energy
To filter
Into all aspects of life
Thereby bringing
Peace and Harmony
To those who need it
Whether they are known to you
Or not.

Blessings to all.

4TH JULY

The time has come
To reassess your life
Looking for the good
And for your Blessings
For there are many.
So gaze upward
Knowing that
Light and Love
Are constantly flowing
Down to you
In an endless stream.
Therefore always be thankful
For what is Now.
Understanding that change will happen
Know these words to be True:
"Love never stands still
But is always expanding"
Thus making it
The Ultimate Gift.

                              Blessings to all.

5TH JULY

Do you walk quietly
And with Love?
For that is the reason
For all of existence.
Know that you yourself
Are the conduit
For Love
And by moving gently
Through your daily life
You contribute
To the general well-being of all.
So stop.
Look around you
And you will see
The many ways
In which you have touched others.
Be aware
And continue surrounding all
With the Gift of Love.

                                    Blessings to all.

6TH JULY

The time has come for action
Albeit
In a large or small way
But positive change
Must surely begin.
So look in your world
At what needs to be dealt with
And then start the process.
Remember to do so
With Love
For any other means
Will bring distress to all.
So slowly
With patience
Start the turning
And you will see
The benefits.
Remember:
Always with Love
Then watch the changes develop.

Blessings to all.

7TH JULY

What is Silence?
Is it empty?
Or are there many worlds within it?
It is from Silence
That all things come
And it is to Silence
That all things go.
So stop.
Listen.
Join yourself
To the peacefulness of Silence
Then from there
Allow yourself to expand
To be fulfilled
And in that Space of Love
Know who you truly are.

Blessings to all.

8TH JULY

What is it that you are looking for?
Is it internal or external?
Or a combination of the two?
For one must establish
A positive position in this world.
Therefore allow your base to be
As solid as possible.
Let all tremors pass
Knowing that your Faith is unshakable.
In this way
The rigors of this existence
Will move away from you
And you will be able
To walk a straighter pathway
Leading you to your goal
Which is an Inner realization of Love.

Blessings to all.

9TH JULY

Come
Listen to your Heart.
Let all else
Fall away
For within you
Are all of the teachings
That you will ever need.
So sit
Allowing the stillness to grow
Then in that Silence
There comes the Voice of Love.
Be aware.
Take note.
Consider
Then act.
Do so in Love
Without fear
So that you may grow
And by doing so
Give Love to all.

Blessings to all.

10TH JULY

At each stage of your life
You are presented with a challenge.
However it is never so great
That you cannot overcome it.
Therefore greet all events
In the spirit of learning
For without such moments
You would not grow
Or develop.
So face each opportunity
With Love
And let that enable you
To become your True Self
Allowing you to expand
Into Love
And become Love.

Blessings to all.

11TH JULY

So it shall come to pass
That all things shall change.
Remember this:
There is no need
To hold onto the past
For by doing so
You are preventing yourself
Moving into a positive future.
So be still.
Take a breath
Then move onward
Letting the past
Go with Love
And with Love
Accepting the new
So that your future is filled
With Hope and Joy.

                                    Blessings to all.

12TH JULY

Walk quietly and gently
For what is the purpose
Of making great noise?
Is it to attract others?
Or to boost oneself?
Either way
It is not necessary
For by walking silently
You can move freely
Focusing on that
Which needs to be done.
And by taking time
You can understand all situations
Allowing positive actions for all.
So understand this:
That all is Love
And with Love
All can be achieved.

Blessings to all.

13TH JULY

Open all of the doors and windows of your mind.
What do you recognize there?
Is it yourself that you see
Or does a stranger live within?
Hiding in the shadows
Feeding from the negative
Aspects of your life?
If so
Face all.
Come to know yourself.
Go through each facet
So that one by one
Each will be polished and cleansed
Allowing that you may shine
Freely and openly
No longer containing doubt and fear
But a beautiful reflection
Of your True Self
A shining Light
To go forward
Joining with others
Bringing Truth and Love to your world.

Blessings to all.

14TH JULY

Even as you read this
There is uncertainty and fear.
Yet there is no need
For what is fear
But the opposite of Love?
So stop.
Wait for the silence to form
And place yourself
In a space
Filled with Love.
From there
You will understand
More clearly
And be able to move ahead freely
Walking in Love and Light
Sharing this with all.

Blessings to all.

15TH JULY

Once words have been read
They can be forgotten
Yet their essence remains
And can be carried forever.
Therefore remember this
And adjust your reading
To the more positive
And Loving kind
For what you carry with you
Will surely shape your mind
And in time also your body.
Then it will ripple into your relationships.
So take care.
Understand
That all communications
Should start and end
In Love.

Blessings to all.

16TH JULY

How you think
Is of vital importance.
It influences your entire being.
So stop
And evaluate yourself.
Be truthful.
Without blaming others
Consider your mind
And how your thought process works.
Then with Love
Begin to slowly change
All that is needed.
By doing so
You can achieve your goal:
To walk in the Light of Love
With constant awareness of doing so.
Be patient
And change will come.

                                    Blessings to all.

17TH JULY

In your Heart of Hearts
Lies the eternal Truth.
So why look outside yourself?
Do you not know
That to live in Peace
It must come
From the Internal self?
Outside may just have
A brief influence.
How long this lasts
Will depend
On many things
But mainly on
Your willingness to rise above them.
Therefore when you are bothered
By such incidents
Look no further than yourself
Your interaction and reaction
For with Truth
The Light of Love will shine
Through and around you
Enabling you to travel on your way.

                                    Blessings to all.

18TH JULY

Follow what is in your Heart of Hearts
For it is there
That you will find
True Contentment and Peace.
Is this not
What every one
Looks and hopes for?
Yet some look outside themselves
Always thinking that it is
A breath or step away.
These people
Will be in a constant
Place of longing
Unable to find
Comfort and rest.
While others
Who face their Inner fears
Will be able to clear
And refresh
The thought patterns
And allow Loving Kindness
To fill them and then radiate to others.
Work tirelessly towards your goal
Knowing that with each breath
You come closer to Unconditional Love.

Blessings to all.

19TH JULY

If you have come to the end of something
Then it is a new beginning
That follows.
So look to the future
For what you wish to be
And with a light Heart
Go about finding
Your way forward.
For what comes next
Is of greater importance
Than what has been.
Leave behind
The negative.
Move into the Light of Love
Allowing the start
Of the next chapter
Of your Life.

Blessings to all.

20TH JULY

Now is the time
To go forward
So take every opportunity
To move ahead.
Do so with a Heart
Full of Love.
In this way
Your journey
Will be guided
By the Pure Light
That always surrounds you.
Cast away fear.
Have Faith
And in doing so
The way will open for you.
Always work with Love
For that is the only way.

Blessings to all.

21ST JULY

After the Silence and Stillness
Comes movement.
So let the past
Become a memory
That melts into the distance
Which in turn
Is lost among forgotten dreams.
Now is the time
To go forward
To plan
To put into practice
All that you know to be true
To live as close to your own goals
As is possible.
In this way
You will achieve happiness
And Peace of Mind.
Be always ready for the changes of life
And move into them with Love.

Blessings to all.

22ND JULY

Now is the time
For the Light of Love
To bring about the changes.
Will you hold it tightly?
Or will you allow it
To flow through you
Like a never-ending stream
Letting it help
All who enter
Your circle?
For the reason of Life
Is to help others
To bring them closer
To their own Truth.
To turn their heads
Once again towards
Their goal.
In this way
They will once more
Begin their own journey
Which will result
In true Peace and Joy
And they will know
Their place in the world.

Blessings to all.

23RD JULY

Look to see all things
In a different light.
For if you only view your surroundings
From their relationship
To your smaller self
You will miss
Their true meaning and beauty.
Remember:
Each situation
Is a potential learning experience
And each living thing
Has its place
In the balance of nature.
Therefore look and see
Not with your small eye
But with your entire Being.
Know that around you
Is the world that you have drawn to you.
Realize that you are part of it
Thus making your actions
And reactions important
Not only for yourself
But also for the entire Whole.
Go forward with Love.

Blessings to all.

24TH JULY

Is change what you truly desire?
Then would you alter your time
Or would it be yourself
That you wish to be different?
Know that others
Are only responsible for themselves.
It is your responsibility to Self
That is important.
Ask yourself many questions
And absorb the answers.
For how else can you have Understanding
And bring about the positive change
That you strive for?
So go gently
With Love and Compassion
For self and others
Who like you wish to travel
A different pathway.

                              Blessings to all.

From each place
Gather what is right for you
Then silently move onward.
For in each situation
Comes the ability
To learn and grow.
Therefore accept and observe all
Knowing that lessons
Can be learnt
At any time and place.
Consider all of the events
And ponder your reaction.
See your faults and perfections
And from there rise above
The smaller self
Thereby having Understanding
Of Self and others.
In this way your thoughts and actions
Will eventually change
Thus allowing you to give
Love and Compassion to all.

                              Blessings to all.

26TH JULY

Be prepared for change
Allowing yourself to be open.
For what transpires
Is of the utmost importance
To you and those around you.
Each life is linked
So what happens to you
And your reaction to it
Will reverberate to all.
You must think of yourself
As a link in a chain:
Some above you
Holding you tightly
While others below you
Looking to you
For guidance and direction
Even if they do not realize it.
So the chain goes onward
All searching for help
Each having a longing
Which is as yet not answered.
Therefore be light of Heart
Sending Light and Love freely.

Blessings to all.

27TH JULY

All living beings
Need Love.
It is like rain
To the parched earth
Helping all to grow
And feel cherished.
It is through this feeling
That help can be given to all
For by sending Love
The sender recognizes
The potential of another
And the recipient
Knows that they have been
Accepted as an individual
In their own right.
These feeling are important
To allow maximum growth
For it is necessary to learn
How to give
As well as receive.
Therefore look to each person
As a dearly cherished friend.
Send Love
Even if it may not be returned
For such is the meaning of Life.

Blessings to all.

28TH JULY

For Love should be
Like an endless fountain
Flowing freely
For all to partake
If they wish.
To do so
They must draw near
And be willing
Not only to bend
But also offer a vessel
Of acceptance to receive.
They may wish
To hold the flow
Or to let it pass by
But that is their choice
And theirs alone.
The giver is not the receiver
Yet they are linked together
For all time
For without one
How can there be another?
So the circle continues
And in this way
All shall know the balance
And the Harmony of True Love.

Blessings to all.

29TH JULY

For what do you now know of Love?
That it is an essential element
Such as the air and water
Of the planet.
For without it
The flow of positive action
Would cease
And life itself
Would take on
A very different meaning.
Therefore allow yourself
To become part of that Love
And even when you forget
Gently bring yourself back
So that you become
United with its rays.
In this way
You are always refining yourself
While helping others.

                                        Blessings to all.

30TH JULY

To give an example to all
Is not just by word.
It is by deed
That you help
To bring Unity
Back into these times
And by living that way yourself
Others will realize
And emulate it.
In this way
Slowly the change
Will occur
And the heaviness
Shall be lifted
And replaced with Loving Peace.
Let that be your thought
As you go along your way:
To lighten the world
For yourself
As well as others.

                                    Blessings to all.

31ST JULY

Liken your life to a stream:
As you flow along your way
There may be barriers
That try to stop you
But they cannot.
However they may force you
To wait or to go
In another direction for a while
Yet eventually you will find
Your own level.
As you flow so you will
Gather from your surroundings
And be a source of help
To all that you pass by.
For some it will be as nourishment
While others will stay at the periphery
And be content.
Yet none is better than another
For each must become a river of their own
Having their own course to follow.
Therefore let your stream
Be a peaceful one
Full of Love and Light
Moving silently along its way.

Blessings to all.

AUGUST

1ST AUGUST

Just as a dot or space
Is at the centre of a circle
So are you
At the centre of your life.
Therefore do not look to another
To fulfill your needs
But go onward
Learning and relating
To that which has and will
Been shown to you.
By traveling your pathway
With constant awareness
You will be able
To let others come and go
As they should.
This will enable you
To share the Light of Love
Willingly and with Compassion.
So walk slowly
Knowing that all comes at the right time
In the right way.

Blessings to all.

2ND AUGUST

With each word
A message is given.
What is important
Is how you react to it.
If you do not remember
Then what is said
Is of little importance
And cannot last.
But if you take it
Into your life
Then each uttering
Will help and guide you
Through even the darkest hours.
So re-read and learn
For these words will bring
Many changes to many people
And they will in time
Spread to all who are hungry
For help and Loving Kindness.
So know the meaning of each page.
Keep them in your Mind and Heart
So that you may share the words
At the right time in the right way.

                                    Blessings to all.

3RD AUGUST

Wrong doing by one
Affects the whole
For are we not all touched
By our brothers' and sisters'
Thoughts and actions?
Yet the only redress
Is to have Compassion
And Love
These being the greatest
Healers of all.
With Compassion and Love
All is changed and forgiven
And in the forgiving
Freedom is experienced.
So strive to be Compassionate
Sending Love to all beings
Thereby freeing yourself and others
From anxiety and pain.

Blessings to all.

4TH AUGUST

Why is it you seek?
For you could live
A much simpler life
Unworried by such awareness.
Yet you have chosen
To be consciously
Part of the Whole
Therefore what befalls you
Is full of meaning.
It is your willingness
To be unified
With your Higher Self
That will allow you
To have greater Understanding and Wisdom
Of others and their situations.
So realize that by sending Love to all
You yourself become the silent channel
That can aid others
In their own search for the Truth.

Blessings to all.

5TH AUGUST

Let the Light of Love
Shine all around you.
Let it clothe you
And seep within your very being
So that every part of you
Rejoices in the knowledge
Of receiving this special Gift.
In this way
You will bring a freshness
To each new day.
This will allow you
To go forward
With an Understanding
Of your situation
And give you the ability
To help others
As they travel
Along their own pathway
Surrounded by the Light of Love.

Blessings to all.

6TH AUGUST

Let no time pass
That is wasted
For each moment
Holds within itself
A glorious chance
To share the Light of Love.
Therefore rather than
Looking back with regret
Do so with delight
Knowing that you have
Given your very best
Thus allowing Love
To flow freely.
For such actions bring
Peace and Hope
With the promise
Of a meaningful tomorrow
For all of humankind.

Blessings to all.

7TH AUGUST

Let no positive chance be untried
No possibility unexplored
For by trial and correct judgment
You will find what is right for you.
If it is not meant
It will fall away
But you will retain
That which you can use.
If it is meant
It will last
And you will be able
To utilize all that you have learnt.
In this way
There are no mistakes
Just different ways of learning.
So be aware of all that comes your way
Allowing Understanding and Love
To promote the necessary Wisdom
Which will direct you
At the right time
In the right way.

Blessings to all.

8TH AUGUST

Where else
If not from one's Inner Depth
Does the awakening
To Truth come from?
For something touches
Your very being
And allows a chord
To be played.
This in turn
Has the ability
To start a symphony
Which will fill you
With Wonder and Joy.
This music shall last you
All the days of your life
Being with you constantly
Sometimes playing louder than others
But always audible to you
When you have ears to hear.
Such is the glorious rhythm
Of the Gift of Love.

                                        Blessings to all.

9TH AUGUST

The very centre of one's Self
Is perfectly still.
Therefore let others
Rush past you
Keeping yourself silent
For they do not know
And can only learn
By your own example.
Let no one break your Stillness.
If perturbed
Wait
Until you have regained it
For it will be a source
Of nourishment
For your Body and Mind.
When you are fulfilled again
You will be able to go forward
Slowly and silently
Sharing Love and Light
With all those you meet
Along your pathway.

Blessings to all.

10TH AUGUST

From new beginnings
Changes may occur.
Therefore let each new day
Bring with it its own freshness
Leaving behind
What was yesterday's.
In this way
With full awareness and Love
You may choose
Either to receive
Or to refuse
That which presents itself.
By allowing each to be considered
On its own merit
And not on some preconceived thought
That which in itself
Holds no meaning
Will easily fall away
And that which remains
Will be cultivated.
Therefore be at Peace.
Be open to the rays of Love
And all will develop
As and when it should.

Blessings to all.

11TH AUGUST

Each day is a step towards your goal.
By having this thought
Whatsoever transpires
Will bring Peace and Harmony.
Therefore look no further
Than today
For what is tomorrow is unknown
And what was yesterday has passed.
Dwelling on both
Will only waste energy
But today well spent
Allows each second
To provide its own wealth
Bringing many gifts.
So live each moment
To the full
Always giving your best.
In this way
That which will become your yesterdays
Can enrich your tomorrows.

Blessings to all.

12TH AUGUST

Humans must go through many stages
Before they can fully understand
The meaning of Life.
To do so they must learn
Life's lessons.
Unfortunately most learning
Is achieved by difficult realizations.
There are many
Who do not wish the hardship of growth
But have chosen to take
The apparently easy pathway.
Although time may pass
Eventually even they
Must travel the road to Wisdom.
It is then with Love
That others who have gone before
Can aid them on their journey.
So know that all is a chain
And no experience is wasted.
For those who once lingered
Can use their Understanding
To guide others
Who like themselves
Hesitated on their pathway.

Blessings to all.

13TH AUGUST

Let your days begin with Stillness
So that you may
Be set on the correct course.
In this way
You will hold the thought of Love
In your Heart and Mind
And all of your actions
Will be filled with Compassion.
Ask nothing for yourself
But have Faith and trust
Knowing that all will be provided
As and when it is needed.
Therefore walk slowly and quietly
Sending Love to all
For this is the only true way
Of union with the Light.

Blessings to all.

14TH AUGUST

Blank pages are for filling.
In the same way
Lives are for living.
It is what you choose
To put into them that matters.
Once you have reached a stage
Where you are aware
Then the responsibility is yours.
You may either
Go forward or not.
To go forward
Means a life of correction
And one of Trust.
To stay still
Means that you
Have reached the end
Of what you wish to be.
So think on these words
And then decide
On your actions.
Do so with Love
So that you may realize
The true workings
Of all that is.

Blessings to all.

15TH AUGUST

Yes, you have Understanding
Or so you say.
It is when the tide of life
Runs against you
That you will know
The depth of your conviction.
Therefore look on each incident
Not as isolated events
But rather as part of a sequence
That will strengthen your Understanding
And give you Wisdom.
So look towards
The Light of Love
And allow its rays
To penetrate deep within
And by so doing
You will be helping
Not only yourself
But also those around you.
For each must face
Their own past
To allow a smooth movement
Into their future.

                                    Blessings to all.

16TH AUGUST

Look to yourself.
Penetrate into your deepest level
Then breathe gently.
Let the Love that is there
Slowly spread
Through your entire Being.
Wait
Until you become aware
Of Love filling every pore
And the calmness
That Love brings.
Then you can proceed
With your day
Certain in the knowledge
That whatever happens
Is for the good.
Know these words to be True:
"That Love holds the key to life
And all else is a continuum."
Therefore hold Love within
Then let it radiate
Outwards to all
Thereby fulfilling your role in the Universe.

Blessings to all.

17TH AUGUST

What is meant by the word worthy?
Do you consider yourself
To be worthy?
For all are worthy.
There is no difference
In the Inner-most reaches
Of every person.
Yet some choose to ignore
Their basic fundamental Being.
This Being consists of Love
Which fills then reaches out
To all.
When Inner Love is forgotten
It becomes harder
To give to others.
When Inner Love is remembered
It flows unconsciously to all.
Therefore know that you are
Primarily made of Love
And allow Love to be given freely
At all times to all Beings.

Blessings to all.

18TH AUGUST

Do not wait for the future.
For it will find you
Whether you wait or not
For every breath takes you there.
So recognize this Truth:
"That time
Once made by human thought
Can either be your friend
Or not."
Therefore greet each moment
With Joy and Love
For it offers you
The opportunity
To bring great positivity
Into your life
And into the lives of others.
By knowing this
All will become a Blessing for the world.

Blessings to all.

19TH AUGUST

What greater Gift can you bring
    Than Love?
For even when
You can do no physical movement
You can send Love.
This will be received silently
And even without awareness
Can be accepted.
Love will help to lift
And to regenerate
Each one who receives it.
Therefore have Faith
In the wonderful healing ability
Of Love.
Make this your goal:
To quietly send Love
To all living beings
Whether animal
Vegetable
Mineral
Or human
For all need Love to exist.

                    Blessings to all.

20TH AUGUST

It is not for you to question
The turning of the seasons.
Likewise it is not for you
To question the outcome
Of your actions
For your behavior will bring
Its own results.
Therefore know this to be True:
"That you alone are responsible
For what befalls you."
You always have the chance
To act with Love.
Even in the hardest times
Love will help
To soften the situation
But more importantly
It will keep you as you should be:
As an extension of Love.
For only when the Light of Love
Shines on all things
Can the Truth be known.

Blessings to all.

21ST AUGUST

What matters to you?
What do you hold most dear?
Then ask yourself
What is important?
The answer is simple:
Love.
For when you can give Love
Your world changes.
It allows you to be Whole.
Even if your Love
Goes unnoticed on the outer level
At the most important level
It is known.
So give your Love freely
To all.
And without trying or looking
Love will find you
And bring with it
The most precious Gift of all:
The ability to share
Love.

                                    Blessings to all.

22ND AUGUST

Is today what you are looking for?
Or is tomorrow
The one that holds
All of your dreams?
Surely today is the one
That holds your future.
Therefore allow each new day
To hold the promise of all things.
In this way you will discover
True Joy.
So live in the Now
And release the past
For by not clinging to it
You will free yourself
From wasting time
By useless worry.
The future is made up
Of each Now
So spend each moment as a Gift
Enjoying and adding with Love
The ability to share with others.
In this way you will vibrate
Harmony to all around you
And in doing so
Spread Love to the world.

Blessings to all.

23RD AUGUST

All things change
Yet remain the same.
Seasons come and go in circles
And you yourself
Grow in circles also.
So look to this present day
To see what lies ahead
Then realize
That you have the ability
To bring about
A golden future.
This will happen
If you wish it to.
Simply by allowing yourself
To be filled with Love
You will know
Inner Peace and Harmony.
Therefore allow Love
To be with you always
A permanent Gift
For yourself and others.

Blessings to all.

24TH AUGUST

Like all things
Love can be on many levels
Yet it is the only constant.
Sometimes it is forgotten.
Sometimes it is no longer used.
But Love is always there.
So remember Love
When you wake.
Remember Love
When you go through your day.
Remember to give Love to all
Regardless of their position
In your life.
And remember Love
Before you sleep
Making each moment
Of your life
A time of true Blessings
For you
And all others.

Blessings to all.

25TH AUGUST

How can you doubt?
For at every moment
You are surrounded
By many Blessings.
Look around you:
See the colours of nature.
Even in dark skies
There are several shades
To be seen.
When after storms
There comes sunshine
So too in your life
When trouble and fear come
They do not stay
But move on.
It is how you experience these moments
That holds the key
To a greater Understanding.
By allowing them to pass
And seeing them as lessons
Your Life's colours
Will be brighter
More harmonious
And filled with Love.

                              Blessings to all.

26TH AUGUST

Do not underestimate
The true power of Love
For it is the energy
That holds the world together.
Each and every one of you
Are in your own world
And for Love to flow freely
You must first
Know and feel it.
Once known
It can then be given to all.
Start with those closest to you
And then radiate Love
On a larger scale.
By doing so
You will help
To heal the past
Of your world
And that of others.
So have patience.
Should you forget
Love yourself first
Then others will feel the Love
That you send
Without the need of words.

Blessings to all.

27TH AUGUST

As it is written
So it stands.
For when spoken
Words cannot be taken back.
They leave an imprint
In the ether
And on the minds
Of all who read and hear them.
Therefore let your words
Be of Loving Kindness
Giving hope to all.
This is the purpose of humankind:
To help
To encourage
And to bring
The Light of Love
To the inhabitants of earth
Whether they be in many life forms
For Love is felt and acknowledged
By all living beings.
So spread Love
With each and every thought
To aid the bringing
Of Harmony and Peace.

Blessings to all.

28TH AUGUST

Open your Heart
For how else can you receive Love?
By being aware of the best
In all things
You will come to see the Light
In each Being
Thereby allowing and giving
The opportunity for all to shine
And become their Higher Self.
This in turn
Will bring about
A happier situation for all.
So first look to Self.
See your worth and value
Then allow those attributes
To be shared.
This will increase and promote
A greater Understanding
In all who know you.
So send and share Love.
For that is your purpose
And your Gift.

Blessings to all.

29TH AUGUST

There are no mistakes
If you learn from them.
So even if you feel
That events are not
As they should be
Look to your words
Thoughts and deeds.
Then with an honest Heart
Prepare to make the necessary changes.
Do so slowly
And with Love
As much for yourself as others.
When this is accomplished
You will find the answers
And be able to go forward
With Love and Understanding
Which brings
A Lightness of Being
To yourself and others.

Blessings to all.

30TH AUGUST

If you were not asked
To go beyond
Your own version of comfort
You would stay
In the same place
Without the chance of becoming
A vessel for Wisdom and Understanding.
Therefore look to your challenges
With Love.
Having Compassion for all
See events from each point of view
And from there
Make your decision.
Know these words to be True:
"That with each time of growth
You move closer to remembering
That who you really are."
So accept with Love
And do only your best
For what else can be asked of you?

                                        Blessings to all.

31ST AUGUST

It was by Love
That all creation was made.
Therefore as each of your thoughts
Becomes a reality
So too does Love flow.
Therefore ensure that your thoughts
Emanate from the home of Love
Thus allowing positive growth.
In this way
All that emerges
Will be for good
And will bring with it
Its own Harmony of Being.
Therefore contemplate Love.
Fill yourself with Love
Until you become
The essence of Love itself.
Allow it to shine forth
Lighting your pathway.
In so doing
You can aid others to see
Their own way forward
Thereby helping to bring
Light to the world.

                          Blessings to all.

SEPTEMBER

1ST SEPTEMBER

What is your wish?
Is it only for yourself
Or does it include others?
For happiness and health
Should be shared
And Love
Should be given to all.
Each day brings
A new chance
To give Love.
Such a simple thing
Yet that alone makes it
The hardest to do.
Therefore encourage Love
To be part of your everyday awareness.
As you breathe
Let Love flow in and out
Filling you
Then traveling to others.
In this way
You will be renewing
The most precious of Gifts.

Blessings to all.

2ND SEPTEMBER

If you could change one thing
What would it be?
Is it something of yourself?
Or do you wish to change others?
For changing others
Means that you are looking
Outward first
Instead of looking inward.
For it is yourself
That you should change.
In doing so
You will inevitably
Find change in others.
For by looking deeply at self
Then improving
You will deal differently
With the world.
This will bring Compassion
And Understanding to all
Allowing Love to flow silently from you
Surrounding others with comfort.
So look within
Then send Love
And change will develop
For the betterment of all people.

                                Blessings to all.

3RD SEPTEMBER

How do you send Love?
Is it by large gestures
With much noise
To attract attention?
Or can it be so silent
And quiet
That the only person
Who knows is you?
Yet the recipient feels
As though their world
Has lifted
And they themselves
Become lighter
In thought and deed.
Therefore in this way you are free
To send Love to all:
To those closest to you
And to those
Whom you may never meet
For Love knows no boundaries.
It is carried in the air
And reaches all.
So remember this
And send Love to the entire world.

Blessings to all.

4TH SEPTEMBER

Such is the way of humankind
That you forget to give thanks
For the times of plenty
Yet in times of sorrow and loss
You remember to ask for help.
This is how it has always been
So for you to break the habit is hard.
Therefore when you receive the gifts
That bring pleasure
Remember to give thanks.
If you do not at the time
Then do so at the end of each day
By saying a silent thank you
And sending Love
And if necessary asking for forgiveness
In case there be cause.
In this way
You will remember your Blessings
And strive to only do good deeds
Thereby adding to the positive flow
Of Loving Kindness.

                                    Blessings to all.

5TH SEPTEMBER

Now is the time
To review your life
So that you can
Really appreciate what you have
For only too often
Can life be taken for granted.
Therefore look around you.
Stop and contemplate
All that you see
From the smallest
To the largest Blessing
For even the least of your Gifts
Deserves thanks.
So send a loving "Thank You"
And strive to act accordingly.
This will lighten your life
Bringing Comfort and Joy
To those around you
Letting loving ripples
Flow from you to all.

                                        Blessings to all.

6TH SEPTEMBER

Today is the start of your life.
No matter what has happened before
This first breath is the new beginning.
Knowing that each breath
Can bring positive change
Look towards every moment
Deciding what it will bring.
For the promise of hope
Is there for you
Allowing you to move forward
With courage and strength.
By moving with Love
You will blaze
A new pathway
That will lead you
To a certainty of Being.
For Love is your True Self.
So honour that spark
And let it light your way.

Blessings to all.

7TH SEPTEMBER

Situations come and go.
What is constant is your True Self.
This Self is connected
To a higher Energy
Than your everyday self.
So during the day
Remember who you really are
And what it is that you wish for.
Notice how you are reacting
To your situation.
Can you truly say
That it is coming from your Higher Self?
This Self would act with Love
Opening up ways that bring Peace to all
Or turning with Love
To leave situations
To find their own loving solutions.
By sending Love
You allow freedom to exist
And new openings to develop.

Blessings to all.

8TH SEPTEMBER

From within
Comes a voice of Peace and Love
Yet it is only found in Silence.
Therefore the everyday noise
And bustle of life
Can sometimes drown it out.
By slowing down
And allowing your mind
To become quiet
You will once again
Hear what is called
"The Sound of Silence."
By doing so
You will understand
Your True Self
And will be able to act accordingly
Letting all heated moments pass
So that you may
Join with Love
To extend it to all of Creation.
Practice.

                              Blessings to all.

9TH SEPTEMBER

To find happiness
Just look within.
What do you find there?
Is it a yearning
For an external answer?
Or is it a place
Where Love abounds?
For there can only be
True happiness
Where the Internal self
Can be linked to the greater Self.
Therefore look to experience Love
Finding Love in nature
And in other meaningful things around you.
By doing so
You will be fulfilled
And Love can sit in your Heart
Allowing you to become a vessel
Of pure Love
Radiating to all.

Blessings to all.

10TH SEPTEMBER

What cannot be forgotten
Can be understood
By knowing the human condition.
Each of you
Has within them
The possibility of great things
But as the ability
To do good is there
So is the ability
To harm others.
Therefore the choice is yours:
Either to grow in Love
Or to decline with negativity.
You are urged to grow
For by hurting others
You yourself know pain.
By holding on to the negative
You will become brittle and hard.
So choose Love over all
Allowing yourself
To rise above
The basic question
Of who to be
And live a full life.

                                    Blessings to all.

11TH SEPTEMBER

From this day
There is a need
To remember who you are
And your connection.
In this way
You will find the pathway
That will help your Understanding
Of the reasons for Being.
When you forget
Go back to the beginning
Of your experience
And recall
All that has happened.
Ask yourself
Is it co-incidence
Or is there an overall pattern?
Then return to your day
And continue to send Love
Silently to all.

Blessings to all.

12TH SEPTEMBER

Days make up weeks
Weeks make up months
Months make up years.
And so it is
That time passes.
Yet you overlook
The seconds and minutes
Of your days
For it is at these times
That great events happen.
At each moment in your life
There is a responsibility to bring Love
Not just for yourself
And others around you
But for all.
In this way
You can add
Wonder and meaning
To your world
Helping all to blossom and grow
Into their full potential
For Love is the nourishment
Of all life forms.

                                    Blessings to all.

13TH SEPTEMBER

Humankind will forever probe.
Their minds will not rest.
They see themselves as master
Instead of guardians
Of the world.
Therefore there can be no Peace
Either with nature
Or fellow human beings
Until they recognize
The need to grow in Harmony
With all of their surroundings.
When this happens
A new dawn
Will open Minds and Hearts
To a harmonious existence
Between all.
This will come
With the realization
Of the true meaning
Of the word
Love.

Blessings to all.

14TH SEPTEMBER

Trust is the most important belief
    For without it
There can be no hope.
Yet it is taken for granted
That night will follow day
And seasons will turn
From one to another.
But in their life
People do not trust
Their own ability
For goodness.
They first rely
On others to show the way
Only then do they react.
Surely each must make the first move
To allow Loving Kindness
To blossom
Thereby spreading Love
In ever-widening circles
Until it encompasses
The entire world.

Blessings to all.

15TH SEPTEMBER

Silence is Golden.
For in that moment
You have the ability
To bring into your life
That which is needed.
You may react to another's words
By instantly replying
Yet that comes without thought
Of either situation or Self.
Therefore by pausing
Time will be given
For small self to fade
And for your True Self
To evaluate all aspects
And to bring a reply
Or to allow a longer silence.
It is not a question
Of being smarter
But of responsibility to Self
For are you not here to develop
And to travel along your pathway?
Therefore, hold silence
And know Peace and Love.
For in this rests
The golden Light.

Blessings to all.

18TH SEPTEMBER

Duty comes before pleasure
For some acts must come first
So that what is necessary
May take place.
Therefore look into your Heart of Hearts
And know where your action lies
For others cannot do your task
Or you take on another's responsibility.
Know these words to be True:
"Work diligently towards
Fulfilling your own goals.
Then when you have awareness
You may pass it on to others."
Work slowly
And in Peace and Love
For in this way
Lies the ability
For personal growth
And helpfulness for others.
Sit - Breathe
And all shall be revealed
So that you may continue
Along your pathway.

                                      Blessings to all.

19TH SEPTEMBER

Do you hear your own music?
Can you allow yourself
The space to dance to it?
Or do you miss it completely?
For each of you
Has your own special tune
One that is created for you alone.
Yet most miss this wonderful rhythm
And try to live
To one that is not theirs
And then wonder why
They are uncomfortable
With life and the people in it.
It is because
They have chosen
To ignore that which is at
The very centre of existence:
"The music of Life."
For even in the outer corners of the universe
Music can be heard.
So listen
To that which is
Played with Love
And enjoy the dance.

Blessings to all.

20TH SEPTEMBER

Humans can change
If they have a Heart to
For that is where the earnest wish
Must come from.
It is indeed
A heart-felt desire
To be able to alter one's Being
And unless the Heart leads the way
Inner conflict could lead
To the reverse happening
And in extreme cases
Illness developing.
Therefore true change
Is not just a mental approach
But Mind
Heart and Body
All moving in the same direction
With the same wish.
In this way
Change will begin to flow
Naturally and easily
So that in time
There will be a new way of Being.

Blessings to all.

21ST SEPTEMBER

Be filled with Peace and Love
For these things above all else
Will help you fulfill your goal.
It is only when
You can truly say
That you understand Stillness
And that you Love your fellow humans
That Peace can flow through you
And you are free of mental conflict.
This will lead you
To a detached view of events
That concern you
And those around you.
By having this approach
You will not be cold
But be able to understand
Each side of the situation
And with Clarity and Love
Help to bring Peace
To all involved.

                                        Blessings to all.

22ND SEPTEMBER

Become an observer
In the play of life.
Step back
For by being too close
You yourself will become involved
And be unable to help.
Therefore be Peaceful
And send Love to all
Allowing them to walk
Their own pathway.
Know that you have a supportive role
And nothing else.
So send a Blessing
Then retire giving them
Their own time and space
For such is the correct way.
Know these words to be True:
"That all happens as it should
When the person is ready
For the next stage
Of their Understanding."
Therefore go quietly
And allow matters to unfold
As they should.

                              Blessings to all.

23RD SEPTEMBER

Look no further than Self
For it is there
That your world begins
Regardless of your surroundings
And actions by others.
It is only your Self
That holds the key
To a happy existence.
How you act
Is the only important factor
For by reacting to others
You lose control of yourself
And of events.
So stop.
Question you own responses
And consider Love in all forms.
Then begin again
With Understanding and Compassion
And by coming from the Silence within
You will only radiate Love.

Blessings to all.

24TH SEPTEMBER

Even when times are hard
Look inward
And ask yourself
How you should react?
What is the proper way to think?
Then act upon your reply
For acting in haste
Or trying to manoeuver events
Will only bring further pain.
So reach deep inside.
Find that place of Stillness
And wait for a growing strength.
In this way
You will allow movement
In the correct direction
Acting instead of reacting
Allowing yourself to receive
The benefits of Contentment and Joy
For Love brings its own reward.

                                Blessings to all.

25TH SEPTEMBER

Whenever others irritate you
Look to yourself.
At first you might not see
A reflection
But wait and look again.
For it is usually
That which you dislike in others
Is that which you wish to hide
In yourself.
Therefore stop.
Be truthful
And if you see the reflection
Understand that this person
Is a Gift
So give thanks and send Love.
Even if you cannot see yourself
Have Compassion
And send Love.
In this way
Both will benefit
From the meeting of Selves.

Blessings to all.

26TH SEPTEMBER

Why wait?
Be prepared for the best to come.
By doing this
You will allow
That which is for you
To reach you and unfold.
So open to the Gift of Hope.
Let your Heart be filled with Love
And from there
Let Love flow through you
Until you overflow.
Then move slowly
Through your days
Knowing that Like
Attracts Like
And that Loving Kindness
Is your true source of Being.

                                        Blessings to all.

27TH SEPTEMBER

What comes from your Heart
Is written on your face
And is in your actions.
Therefore look deeply and question
Your deepest wishes
For perhaps when you look deeper
The Truth is not in your Heart
But in your Heart of Hearts.
At the deep level of your Being
Your True Self lies
And it is from there
That the real Truth sits.
Sometimes it is hidden
By the rush of everyday life.
Sometimes it speaks to you
And you do not listen.
So be still
Allowing Love to expand
From your Inner Being
And follow that radiant Light
Walking on the pathway of Love.

Blessings to all.

28TH SEPTEMBER

Let Heart and Mind move you
For it is from these two places
That the Truth will come.
For deep inside you lies
That which cannot be ignored
And to go against it
Will bring uncertainty and discomfort.
So consider both
Then moving slowly
Tread your chosen pathway
With the Knowledge and Understanding
That such awareness brings.
Be patient and Loving with others
Allowing them to travel
Either with you or not
For by sending Love to all
Each will find their own way
Helped by the silent Radiation
Of your Love and Compassion.

                              Blessings to all.

29TH SEPTEMBER

What lies within is hidden
Even from yourself
For it is only in times of questioning
That you are called upon
To go to that deep place
Where your True Self is found.
There is the source of your Being
And from there you will find
The way to Be.
Therefore look to such times
As a Blessing
For by not knowing the overview
You cannot understand
Why events unfold.
Yet by acting from your Self
Which is the home of Loving Kindness
You can be confident of the outcome.

Blessings to all.

30TH SEPTEMBER

When you are young
You spend time asking "why?"
Yet as you grow older
That question fades
And as your life unfolds
So does the wonder of the answers.
In youth you see
More hope and promise
Yet this can be forgotten
As dreams are not realized.
So stop
And remember your dreams.
See if life has unfolded
For the best
Giving you a more stable
And loving reality.
For what would you really change
With the Understanding
Of what needed to be learnt?
Surely the easiest path was trodden
And you were always held
In loving Hands.
Therefore be thankful
And proceed with Love.

Blessings to all.

OCTOBER

1ST OCTOBER

To be able to give Love
You must firstly
Know Love from within.
For how else
Can you radiate
And send Love to all?
So look within.
Fill yourself with Love.
Let it reach every part
Of your Being.
Then and only then can you
Send Love to all
For this is the purpose
Of humankind:
To choose Love and share it.
So ponder on these words
And know them to be True:
"First know Love yourself
Then you will be free of all doubt
And be able to live and walk
In its glorious Light."

Blessings to all.

2ND OCTOBER

Let go of past events
For what good
Can come of reliving happenings?
Rather look forward
Moving into the future
Taking only that which can help
And enlighten you.
In this way
Whatever comes
You will be equipped
To act accordingly
Relying on your learning
And experience.
Then with an open Heart
Let Love shine through
Into each situation
Thus bringing the ability
To work within
The Light of Compassion
For the good of all.

Blessings to all.

3RD OCTOBER

Love that is found in your Heart
Can be subjective.
Therefore look deeper
Into your Heart of Hearts
For there it is true and pure.
It does not rely on others.
It does not judge
Or compare
But flows freely to all.
So know this to be True:
"Love itself is free from boundaries.
It surpasses all
And reaches into the furthest corners
Of Being."
So practice sending Love
And soon it will become
A natural happening
Without any effort.

Blessings to all.

4TH OCTOBER

If you are in doubt
Wait
For in time events
Will make themselves evident.
Then with a full Heart
Go forward slowly.
Haste in most matters
Can bring regret
So what is needed
Is Patience and Love.
When you are still
And filled with Love
Situations take on a different meaning
And you can deal appropriately
With your surroundings.
Each one of you
Is called upon
To exercise Love
And how you do so
Will determine
Your pathway in life.
So put Love first.

Blessings to all.

5TH OCTOBER

Be full of Love
For by doing so
You align yourself
With your future.
As you think
So you become.
This is true for your mental
And physical Being
Therefore it is of the utmost importance
That you hold this premise within you.
By constant practice
This will become easier to achieve
And will be a natural state for you.
Know these words to be True:
"That you and you alone
Hold the key to a joyous Life."
So begin today
Slowly unfolding
And allow Love to blossom
From your Heart of Hearts.

Blessings to all.

6TH OCTOBER

From the beginning of time
Humans have seen the stars
And have striven to conquer them.
This in itself
Has been their failure
For in such striving
Unity is lost.
Therefore they should seek
The unity in all things
Whether it be internal or external.
The important goal is Harmony.
When this is achieved
Wisdom will prevail
And Love will abound.
Then all will be realized.
Therefore look no further
Than yourself
For in this way
Once you have Inner Harmony
You will be able
To go forward
With the Light of Love.

Blessings to all.

7TH OCTOBER

The connecting factor in life
Is Love.
It is the driving force
That allows you to rise
Above the baser levels.
It is the gentle energy
That brings balance.
It is the Divine Essence
That allows you to Unite
With your Higher Self.
Therefore be at Peace.
Cultivate Love
In its purest form
For in this way
Your steps will always
Be in the right direction
And you will know
Harmony and Serenity of Mind.
Let Love - true Love
Be your guide.
Open your Heart
Disregarding all else
So that you may walk
In its glorious Light.

Blessings to all.

8TH OCTOBER

"What you put into your life
Is what you will receive."
Think long on these words
For they hold within them
The Wisdom of all ages.
From these simple words
You have a guiding line
That will lead the follower
To the Truth.
By acting upon this
Life is transformed
From the accidental
To the direct
For no deed
Will go unnoticed.
Therefore always remember
To act accordingly.
In this way
As you reap the benefits of your actions
You will know that they are truly deserved
And you will be able to share
The Light of Love
With others.

Blessings to all.

9TH OCTOBER

Lift your heart.
Allow Light and Love
To flow through you.
Then having given thanks
Continue with your daily work
So that you may spread Love
To all
Not verbally unless asked
But more so by example.
Have only kind words
And good deeds
And a listening ear.
In this way
You will not judge
But encourage all
Who come into your circle
To realize the Truth
And to travel
Like you
Their own pathway.

> Blessings to all.

10TH OCTOBER

So long as there is Light
There will always be darkness.
Therefore be not dismayed
But look beyond the darkness
Seeking the Light.
Then having found it
Allow its rays to reach outward.
In this way
Much will be received
And as you move into
Its glorious Radiation
You will gain strength.
This will allow you to deal
With the elements of life.
Knowing that all is for the purpose of betterment
You will become stronger in your beliefs
And have the ability to hold Compassion and Love
For those who unlike yourself
Exist without direction.

Blessings to all.

11TH OCTOBER

If you are Still
At your centre
Then the outside world
Will not worry you.
Therefore watch and listen.
Observe as if in a play
Knowing that the lines
That have been said
Do not always
Hold true meaning.
In this way you will know
What to believe in
And what to let pass by
Thus allowing your centre
To always be protected.
Even if turmoil comes close
Be still and ask for guidance
And with a true Heart full of Love
You will be granted
What is rightfully yours.

Blessings to all.

12TH OCTOBER

Let no stone be unturned
For what lies buried
Must be brought
To the Light
Even if it means facing
That which you do not wish to.
For what is hidden
Has a hold
And what is revealed
Can be set free.
Therefore be brave
In your dealings.
Seek the truth
In all aspects of self
And with constant awareness
Compassion and Love
Change will come
Thus allowing you to travel
Further along your pathway.

Blessings to all.

13TH OCTOBER

For such is the meaning of Life
That all things come
Then pass away.
Nothing remains the same.
So travel along your pathway
Knowing that what is given
Is loaned
And that when the time is right
You will let them go.
So hold no object
Tight in your heart.
Enjoy the Gifts
But do not try to own them
For only those of Self are yours:
They will last with you.
Yet such precious tokens
Are not visible.
They are worn
To be seen
By certain eyes
Who share in your Joy and Love
And also travel their pathway.

                                        Blessings to all.

14TH OCTOBER

Heaven can be here on earth.
It is within your capability
To achieve it.
How you perceive heaven
Is the question.
To most it can never be reached
For they do not have eyes to see.
They look
But do not recognise beauty
Nor can they relate to it
So heaven is always that step away.
Others know Stillness
And understand that beauty
Can only come from within.
Then having experienced it internally
They are able to see
The wonders of the world.
Such vision transforms
This world into heaven.
So simple.
So true.
For it takes Love
To unfold the beauty of all.

                              Blessings to all.

15TH OCTOBER

From what angle
Do you perceive your life?
Is it from a straight road
Or do you allow curves?
The former may bring
Its own heartache
As such a path
Can too easily be lost
Its form being so rigid
That its own expectations defeat it.
Therefore the latter is more acceptable
For although it may appear longer
It is in fact
A gentler pathway
Slowly winding along
Gathering that which has been learned
And using the lessons
Learnt with Love
For the good of all.

Blessings to all.

16TH OCTOBER

For as the written word is read
It may linger.
This in turn
Could make familiar reactions change
So that one is no longer
Held by habit.
For by remembering
You will be free
To go forward.
By allowing this to happen
Even once
Great changes will occur.
For the very structure
Of your Life will alter
And what was once negative
And doubtful
Will become a glorious shining pathway
Full of Encouragement and Hope
Taking you beyond your boundaries
Leading you to the Truth
And into the Light of Loving Kindness.

Blessings to all.

17TH OCTOBER

Stillness can only be held by diligence.
One should always come back to the breath
For how else can you keep contact
With that which is beyond time and space?
Mind must be brought to rest
On No-thing
So that there is an opening
Through which Union is made.
For stillness cannot barge its way through
The constant noise
Of everyday thoughts.
If too much effort is needed
Then a great deal of energy is lost.
So learn how to sit still
And wait to experience emptiness
Allowing that you yourself
May be filled
With Love and Light.

                                        Blessings to all.

18TH OCTOBER

Unfold in your own way
For to try to copy someone else
Will lead to confusion
And doubt about one's self.
Remember it is your own pathway
That must be trod.
Others may show what is possible
But it is you
Who must walk your own.
This can only be done
By practice
And trying all possibilities.
Only then can you make your choice
And follow what is right
And true for you.
Hold on to your Beliefs
Then as you go along
You shall know Peace
And a Quietness
Of an open
Joyous and Loving Heart.

                                        Blessings to all.

19TH OCTOBER

Let Gentleness and Love
Open your heart
For you do not need to be hard
In mind and body
To reach that which
You have set for yourself.
Others may try to change you
But you only need to be centered
And their negativity will pass you by.
Therefore with a Heart
Filled with Love and Compassion
Trust.
Let no one or no thing
Disturb your Truth
Then you shall always be ready
To help others.
This is your goal
Your purpose
So bring yourself to centre.
Radiate from there
And all else shall fall away.

                                        Blessings to all.

20TH OCTOBER

From deep within you
You may hold thoughts
That must be released.
So to help you achieve this
You are placed in situations
That require a change of mind.
Look deeply.
Recognize
Then let go.
This is not a surface change
Smiling while you harbour
Negative feelings
But a true Rejoicing
An uplifting of Heart
An opening of Mind.
Once this has been reached
There will be no fear
Only Love
And with it the ability
To go forward.
So first be still
Thereby gaining
Understanding and Wisdom.

Blessings to all.

21ST OCTOBER

From above come tones of music.
This music is made up of Love.
Each note
Like a ray of sunlight
Penetrates deep within each Being
Giving Light and Love to all.
That is why
The whole of the universe
Is open to, and made up
Of vibrations.
That which you are made from
Is the material of Creation.
You are all the same:
You live
Then are no more
But your vibration
Shall exist forever.
So let Love fill you.
Open your heart
To the music of the Heavens
Then from there go forward
Into the future
Sharing Peace and Love
As you slowly walk your pathway.

Blessings to all.

22ND OCTOBER

Let the Light shine through you
And open your Heart to the Love
That is all around you.
Think not that you are separate
But know that you are One with All.
There can be no distinction
From one to another.
Each one's pain and sorrow
Is shared throughout the Universe.
It is not just empathy:
It is a true sharing.
Joy and Sorrow
Pain and Pleasure:
Each radiates throughout space
Emanating vibrations.
These are felt and acted upon
By the Whole of Creation.
Therefore have the Understanding
And awareness of each of your
Thoughts, Actions and Deeds
Allowing change to develop
Where necessary
So that you add
To the Peace and Joy of the world.

                              Blessings to all.

23RD OCTOBER

Fear not.
Let go
For holding on
To what has gone
Will only lead to useless
Pain and sorrow.
Give gladly of yourself
When needed
Then let all other thoughts pass.
Know that what happens is meant
And shows the state
Of the human consciousness.
You can do no more
Once it has happened
Therefore learn
And then allow your lesson
To penetrate to a deeper level.
Remember:
You can be none other
Than self in Self.
So sit and be still
Allowing the Light of Love
To guide you.

Blessings to all.

24TH OCTOBER

Discipline balances the workings of the Heart.
It has the ability to open
And give Love to all
Regardless of whether
You as an individual
Like them or not
For who are you to judge?
Therefore see all
As travelers along the pathway.
Just as you yourself
Struggle at times
So too do all living beings
Each having their own lessons
To find themselves in
And to work their way out of.
For this reason
Be kind
For what you see in others
Is merely a reflection of self.
So go slowly
Walking quietly
And sending Love to all.

                                        Blessings to all.

25TH OCTOBER

Go through your life gathering smiles
For although tears will come
Let them fall away
Together with thoughts
Of what might have been.
For perfect happiness is found
By living in the Now
And by allowing all things to pass
The laughter and the fears
Can in time be regarded as the same.
Allow that a smile holds
The centre emotion.
Remember with a smile
The great happiness
Of how you overcame your fears.
Yet both have passed on
And you yourself
Are reading this in the Now.
So smile
Knowing by doing so
You add to your strength of purpose
Thereby enabling you to proceed
Into many other Nows
With Love.

Blessings to all.

There is but one way
To live your life
And that is to be
In tune with your Self
To be able to realize
That part of you
Which is linked to the greater Self.
In this way
You will always lean
Towards Light and Love
And all that they stand for.
For in truth how can you walk
Among your fellow human beings
If you know
And do not act
On that wonderful Understanding?
So let your smaller self grow and unite
Allowing that you may put into practice
All that you know to be true
Thereby sharing with all
Who wish to walk
Along their own pathway.

Blessings to all.

27TH OCTOBER

Are you all not as children
Here for your own reasons?
Therefore realize that you
Are in the great school
Of earthly life
Each being a spark
Whose task it is
To travel onward
Drawing ever closer to their goal.
In this way
You are at times
Parent, sibling
Friend and foe
For you all have many roles
And experiences to fulfill.
With this in mind
Open your Heart.
Let Love fill the whole of your Being
So that you can rejoice in such Knowledge.
This will bring Peace and Understanding
For yourself and others around you
Allowing them the freedom
To become
Their True Selves.

Blessings to all.

28TH OCTOBER

Allow each person to travel
Their own pathway
So that by encouraging such movement
The bond that is between you
Will still remain
And in fact
Grow stronger.
For as each grows
A new respect
Will develop
And a greater Understanding
Will strengthen an already
Unshakable Love.
For people unite for a purpose
Which will continue
Throughout their lifetime
Each sharing that which is required.
Such is the meaning of Love:
A gentle giving and receiving
Allowing each to blossom
In their own way
At the right time.

Blessings to all.

29TH OCTOBER

As a new time comes into being
Hold within your Heart
All that has brought you
To this moment
For much has been received
And held dear.
Yet there are new times
To add to the old
Which will allow you to go forward.
Know that nothing stays the same
But where Love is as a foundation
Although things may alter
They will always
Hold to the Truth.
So go quietly
Sending a silent Gift of Love
And allow all to develop
As it should.

Blessings to all.

30TH OCTOBER

Speak only words
Of a positive nature
For only then
Shall you know the meaning
Of the Light of Love.
Let each utterance
Bring people together
Thus showing the way
To heal wounds
And strengthen the bonds
Of friendship and Love.
In this way
You yourself
Will take part
In the healing of the World.
Do so with Gentleness and Compassion
Monitoring each step
So that you are aware
And responsible for yourself.
Although it is not easy
It begins with one word
And with a true Heart
You can slowly be mindful
Speaking only that which might be said
To promote Peace and Love.

Blessings to all.

31ST OCTOBER

Know who you are.
Then you can face the world
And all that it has to offer.
By being your True Self
You will be strong enough
To face all of life's complexities
That may be directed towards you.
It is only by sifting through
Many layers that Self
Can come through.
By not being interested
In labels placed upon you by others
Or thoughts
That you feel you should follow
You will be able to know
What is in your Heart
And that which is True.
Then a pathway
Will be formed
Allowing you to walk slowly
Along its glorious length
Surrounded by the Light of Love
Having Inner Peace and Harmony
Of Being.

                                        Blessings to all.

NOVEMBER

1ST NOVEMBER

It is how you face your disappointments
That is the key to happiness
For in each life
There are times of hardship.
This is inevitable
For how else will you grow
And understand the meaning
Of your life?
Therefore know this to be True:
"Where there is Joy
There is also sorrow.
Where there is light
There is also darkness.
Yet where there is Love
All can be smoothed and comforted."
So go forward with Love in your Being
Allowing Love to filter through
And then overflow to all
Thereby silently helping others.

Blessings to all.

2ND NOVEMBER

It is easier than you think
To walk in the Light
For if you go slowly
You yourself place each foot
Thereby making every step
One that brings you closer
Or takes you further away
From your goals.
Therefore with personal responsibility
And true awareness of Self
Your way is formed
Almost as if it happened
Of its own accord.
Yet what transpires
Will be of the utmost importance
Each event having a deep meaning
For you and others.
Therefore move with Love
Knowing that spreading Light
Brings its own Gifts.

Blessings to all.

3RD NOVEMBER

Awareness of Self
Brings the realization
That you are part of the Whole
For do you not all in your own way
Have an interweaving
With each other's lives?
Then, knowing these words
To be true
Act accordingly
So that you may
Bring unity to all
Who come within your realm.
For such is the way
Of true happiness:
To bring the Light of Understanding
To all
So that they may
Walk firmly on their pathway
Each making their own journey
Towards the Light and Love.

                                    Blessings to all.

4TH NOVEMBER

Where do you find Love?
Is it in others
Or is it in material objects?
Or perhaps you now realize
That Love can only be found
In your Heart of Hearts
For it is there that
Unconditional Love resides.
So when you are in need of Love
For yourself and others
Look there
And know this to be True:
"That without Love
There can be no happiness
Or positive growth."
Therefore when challenged in your life
Remember to turn inwards.
Then finding Love and Peace
Return to your world
And give Love back to all.

                                    Blessings to all.

5TH NOVEMBER

It is said that you must take
The rough with the smooth.
The smooth you will glide over
And when memory releases it
It is gone
While the rough in itself
Will smooth over your edges.
It goes deeper within
And helps to remould you
Thereby being a lasting experience.
To this end
You should look to the rough times
And choose what lasting effect
You wish to gleam from them.
Will you hold a grudge
Or can you grow in Love?
Surely the latter holds the better alternative.
So stop.
Look to your Heart of Hearts
And come from a place of Love
Allowing positive change to happen.

Blessings to all.

6TH NOVEMBER

Perhaps your life experiences
Have made you question yourself.
Yet understand that you are
Where you should be
Doing what you need to do.
When you understand this
You will look deeper into your life.
Each thought and action holds the future.
So travel well.
Ask yourself
What do I need to realize?
Instead of why is this happening to me?
Know these words to be True:
"It is your action not reaction
That holds great importance
And how much Love you give
Is the true measure of your Understanding."

Blessings to all.

7TH NOVEMBER

Hope is a peaceful state.
It is different from a wish
For a wish brings longing
Which in itself holds an external yearning.
Yet hope is an Inner strength
A silent belief
That there will be a positive outcome.
Therefore allow Hope to rest
In your Heart of Hearts.
Let it mingle and unite with Love.
Therefore know these words to be True:
"Hope and Peace abide in Love.
Where there is one
The other silently sits."
So fill yourself with Love
Encouraging every moment
To bring positive change.

                                    Blessings to all.

8TH NOVEMBER

Love is the only Gift
That is necessary
For all else passes.
Yet Love can be given silently
Without anyone being aware
Of the most precious of Gifts surrounding them.
They will only know that they
Feel happier and more comfortable.
So it is that when Love is given
The person sending Love
Will also benefit.
Know these words to be True:
"That Love given is a Blessing to all."
Therefore by understanding this
Your life and others will change forever.

Blessings to all.

9TH NOVEMBER

Be open to the beauty around you
Knowing that to experience it to its fullest
You must first become still.
For in haste and movement
Much is lost.
In Stillness you will recognize
The external beauty
And having done so
Will then internalize it
Making the source of beauty
A reality that will enrich
Your life in many ways
Thus giving you strength
To continue along your pathway.
Open your Heart to Love
And all positive vibrations
Thereby making your days filled
With wonder.
Practice
For even in the smallest movement
You may waste the chance of opening your awareness.
Become peaceful
And all shall be as it should.

Blessings to all.

10TH NOVEMBER

To live your life as you should
You must first know your centre.
This should be strong
And although not rigid, solid
So that you always have a form
To support you.
Therefore do not worry about another's pathway
Or other people's wrongful deeds
For it is for each of you
To work through your own events
Doing what you think is right.
Thus either allowing your pathway
To grow or not
As your actions happen.
Become still.
For you are always connected
To the source of all
Which is Love
And it is from there that you will
Find all that you need
And all that you will become
Will be because of your connection
With the ultimate Reality.

Blessings to all.

11TH NOVEMBER

It is time for bringing
Awareness into your life
For words are empty
If they hold not meaning
In your actions.
So ask yourself:
What do you want from your life?
Then slowly and with Love
Start to bring about
The positive changes.
Walk slowly
So that you move
With as little disturbance as possible.
In this way
You will be sure
That all that comes to pass
Will be accepted with Love.
Have Compassion for those around you
For they are part of your existence
And should be respected as such.

                                    Blessings to all.

12TH NOVEMBER

Words are an important part of life
For they help communication with others
And allow ideas
To spread over great distances.
They also help to spread the Word.
Yet what is the Word?
It is only a singular thought.
From that one Word
Many are formed
All trying to clarify the one.
Therefore misinterpretation may develop
And the central experience is lost.
For when using the Word
Careful thought should be given
To what is said.
Then after having used
The minimum amount of words
Silence should be left to develop
For it is in the space that most
Will find their own true meaning
Thereby being able to experience
The Word
In their own inspired way.

Blessings to all.

13TH NOVEMBER

So many things are going on around you
Yet you have little or no Knowledge of them.
It is because you could not cope
With more than you need to know.
Therefore look to your immediate relationships
And deal with them.
In this way you
Allow events to unfold
In the correct way.
This in turn will encourage
A peaceful existence for all.
Be free of doubt
For by settling your affairs
With a Loving Heart
You will in fact
Bring Peace to many.
This applies to those around you
And to those whom you will never know
Who reside at a great distance from you
Even encompassing the whole world.

Blessings to all.

14TH NOVEMBER

In the world at this time
There is the need to realize
The true meaning of Love
For without Love
There can be no growth
Or positive expression.
Therefore look to yourself
And ask whether you live
In fear or Love.
If it is the former
Find the cause
And give Love to all involved
Either verbally or silently
And wait for change to develop.
By doing this you will allow
All to move forward.
Be brave and Trust
So that you may live in the latter.
Know this to be True:
"By sending Love to all Creation
You yourself are Blessed."
So each day send Love
And by this
Know your role in the universe.

                                        Blessings to all.

15TH NOVEMBER

If there is a time and place
It is Now
For what else do you have
But this moment?
So it is said that
To live in the Now
Is the only way to be.
Yet how hard do you find it?
You are always looking in two directions:
Either behind or ahead.
Know this to be True:
"You only need to look at yourself now
To know your past
And likewise
Your future."
For that which you would like to change
Begins Here and Now.
So start all happenings with Love
For yourself and others
And in doing so great changes will occur.

Blessings to all.

16TH NOVEMBER

Why worry
For what good can it do?
If you know that you have done your best
Then all that is left
Is to wait and let things unfold
As they may.
Be patient
For you do not know
The over-view
And what seems right
In your eyes
May not be.
So where is your element of Trust?
Is it just a word
Or can you really let go
And feel it in your Heart of Hearts?
By accepting Trust
You will become calm
Making your life easier
Thereby being able
To send Love instead of fear
Enabling all to take Place
As it should.

Blessings to all.

17TH NOVEMBER

You are never alone.
Even if you are unaware of it
The Love in Creation
Is always with you.
All comes from the same place.
Each one holds
The same spark
Of essential Being.
Therefore look around you.
Know these words to be True:
"See yourself in everything.
There is no separation
Just Love."
So let yourself
Melt into the ocean
Of Unconditional Love
And become One with the universe.

                                    Blessings to all.

18TH NOVEMBER

Sit and wait
For events to unfold
Without you having to make great effort.
Therefore know these words to be True:
"That it is only in the Being
And not in the doing
That importance lies."
For once you have passed
A certain point
There should be no effort or strain
But all should be allowed
To flow as it should.
You now know the difference
Between positive and negative
Therefore you are in control of your thoughts.
From there actions grow.
This will in itself
Make the difference.
Allowing you
To be moved
In the right direction.
Yet all stems from you
And your wish to say
The right thing for all.

Blessings to all.

19TH NOVEMBER

In the area in which you live
The time which is called a year
Is coming to a close.
Therefore it is a good time
To look back and contemplate
Your thoughts
Words and actions.
How have they materialized?
Is it as you have wished?
What was your role in events?
Or has there been room for improvement?
So stop.
Be Still.
Enter into the Silence of Love
And ask for guidance and clarity.
Then proceed to make the correct changes
To yourself
For by being centered in Love
You can only do your best
Love being all that there is.

                                    Blessings to all.

20TH NOVEMBER

As we all come from the Silence
Where all sound is formed
Ask yourself
Why do you speak?
Is it just for your voice to be heard?
Or does it go deeper in meaning?
For surely there is more to speaking
Than idle chatter.
Know these words to be True:
"Sound itself is made to extend
The Joy of Being
To bring Hope and to encourage Love.
As all comes from the Silence
So all goes back to it."
Therefore allow your words
To be made up of Love
Thereby lifting all round you
To a place of Joy and Love.
Go slowly
And remember the true meaning
Of the spoken word.

Blessings to all.

21ST NOVEMBER

Always let there be room for change
For by holding on to the present
You will restrict all possibilities.
Therefore enjoy the Now
As it is
Or wait having done your best
For events to pass
Knowing that all changes.
In this way you will be free
To really live your time span
To the utmost.
So let your ideas flow
Being filled with Love and Hope.
Know these words to be True:
"That where there is life
There is the ability for Love
And where there is Love
All things are possible
For the bringer of Love."
Even if things are not as you wish
You will find comfort in Love.

Blessings to all.

22ND NOVEMBER

There should be a time
For Stillness and Silence in your day.
To this end
You can place a time in your mind
To allow this to happen
Whether it be in the morning or night.
Yet a time should be set
For contemplation and higher thoughts.
In this way
No matter what happens
You will be brought back
To your True Self
To your very centre of Being.
This will connect you once again
So that you may reunite
And be able to go forward
With Love in your daily life.
Even if you do not think
That you have the time
A short thought will suffice
And you will know
That you are joined
To the never-ending stream
Of Unconditional Love.

Blessings to all.

23RD NOVEMBER

Love is always around you.
It fills the universe
But it is for you to remember
And provide your own Love
To add to it
Thereby making a world
Of Peace and Harmony.
Can you do this?
Can you remember
And in so doing
Send Love to all
Regardless of your own opinion?
For this is True Love
Unconditional and a True Gift.
So restart today
Taking in Love
And gently sending Love
Silently and freely
Uniting your Blessings
To cover the world.

Blessings to all.

24TH NOVEMBER

First know yourself.
By doing so you will know others
For all are One
Each in their own way
Reflections of the many aspects
Of the One.
Therefore be slow to judge others
And their way
For they may have found
That which is right for them.
This should be rejoiced
Allowing them
To move slowly
Along their pathway
Yet at the same time knowing
That perhaps it is not for you.
Be kind.
Know that there are many ways
All leading to the same awareness
Which is contact with the Self
And Unconditional Love.

Blessings to all.

25TH NOVEMBER

Is it not with Love
That you are guided?
Therefore know
That in the hardest of times
Strength will be given.
That you are not alone.
So raise your head.
Hold within your Heart
Life's flame
And allow the true Light
To flow through you.
From there you will be taken
And placed where you are needed most.
In this way
Not only you your Self will grow
But also others around you.
So go forward
Letting the Light shine
Through and from you.

Blessings to all.

26TH NOVEMBER

Lessons are usually difficult to take
Yet they are the ones
Of which the most notice
Should be taken.
So look to yourself
And find the True meaning.
It will be as if
You are looking into a mirror.
The secret is to find
That which you need to learn
And apply it to yourself
For only when you have mastered
The lessons in many ways
Will you be truly free
And be able to move on.
So look deeply within
With Love and Compassion
Then with Understanding
Change that which is needed
To allow you to know
Freedom.

Blessings to all.

27TH NOVEMBER

To understand self
It is advisable to look to your thoughts
For it is there that your actions begin.
Therefore wait
And question where they arise from.
Is it from your Higher Self?
Or do they emanate from ego?
Surely as you are in human form
Ego has a role to play
In experiencing the world
Yet it is only a small part of self.
This needs to be controlled
And by self realization
This can be achieved.
Look closely with Love.
Be gentle on yourself
And move slowly
In your chosen direction
For help is with you
Walking silently by your side.

                                        Blessings to all.

28TH NOVEMBER

What is the Truth?
Is it how you experience it?
Or is it from another's
Point of view?
Surely it must be
Somewhere in the centre
Of each person's awareness.
Therefore look
With Love and Compassion
At each event.
Step back
So that you may have
A wider Knowledge
Then wait for Peace to fill your Being
And only then can you go forward.
So wait
For things may not be as they seem
And know that with Love
All can be achieved.

Blessings to all.

29TH NOVEMBER

From deep within
Let the Light radiate
So that you can illuminate
Not only your own life
But also the lives
Of those who have chosen
To come into the circle
Of your Being.
Therefore Trust
And having lit the flame
Allow it to shine.
Warm and refresh yourself
By its glow
And know that you will be led
Closer to your goal
In the fullness of time.

Blessings to all.

30TH NOVEMBER

At the end of each day
Reappraise it
For in doing so
You will find
Not only your positive actions
But also your failings.
In this way
You will be able
To change your weaknesses
Into constructive lessons
Thereby always working
Towards a positive development.
Although this pathway is not easy
You are not alone.
There are many who walk with you.
Remember that you are surrounded
By glorious Light and Love
And in so doing
You will be a Blessing to others.

Blessings to all.

DECEMBER

1ST DECEMBER

If you had any wish
What would it be?
Would it be for yourself?
Or for others?
Yet stop and ask yourself
Do you really know
What is best?
And do you
Want such responsibility
That you can plan another's life?
Surely it is better to trust
To those that know
Leaving the choice to them.
Therefore send Love
And by doing so
You allow yourself and others
To do the best
That can be done
Without interfering
With the correct flow of Being.

Blessings to all.

2ND DECEMBER

From this time onward
Know that you are One
That all things can be brought together.
What is required of you
Shall be yours to give.
Therefore strive for perfection.
So that you may achieve it
Look no further than your Heart of Hearts
For you know the Truth
And how much you have tried
To maintain it.
Look within.
Let your Inner and outer strength
Melt into one
And use this energy
To bring proper direction
To your movements.
To know is not enough:
To BE is the essence of existence.
Therefore learn
And having absorbed with Love
Put this Knowledge
Into practical Wisdom.

                                        Blessings to all.

3RD DECEMBER

When you send Love
    You soften
Not only your thoughts
But also your body.
Therefore it is beneficial
To both the sender
And the one who receives.
And there is also
Another reason for doing so:
Love is passing through the ether.
As it does so
A certain amount stays
Making a trail of Love
Which will filter throughout space.
In this way
You will help
To bring Healing
Peace and Love
To countless beings
Not only to humankind
But to all of Creation.

                              Blessings to all.

4TH DECEMBER

Lost at the centre
Of your daily life
Is the truth.
Yet you have buried it
Under the fabric
That you have woven for yourself.
So be still
And let pretence
Fall away
For what will be left
Will be your True Self
Which will then
Give you the strength
And the foundation
To go forward
Into the glorious future.
Therefore take Heart.
Listen and learn
Knowing with Love and Compassion
All will be given.

Blessings to all.

5TH DECEMBER

The Truth will be known.
Even if you disguise it
In your own version of events
Eventually you will have to
Face the facts.
Therefore it will save you
Endless energy
If you speak truthfully in the beginning
For if not
You are only fooling yourself
And making others question
Their faith in you.
So even if it is asking
A great deal of yourself
Speak the truth with Love
And watch and wait
For Love to soften
And join together all involved.

                                        Blessings to all.

6TH DECEMBER

Above all know Peace.
For then you may know space
And as you expand
Into openness
So you will begin
To get a glimpse of reality.
By doing this
You will know the Truth:
That all is equal
And in balance
That harmony lies
At the very centre
Of existence.
Therefore as part of the greater plan
Move slowly.
Take your time to know all
Giving each
The same amount of attention.
In this way
You will move forward
Along your pathway
With Love and Compassion.

Blessings to all.

7TH DECEMBER

If there is to be Peace in the world
It must first
Come from the individual
For it is in each Heart and Mind
That the ability
To exist in Harmony materializes.
Therefore by finding Inner contentment
You will begin to bring about
Life-changing events
For yourself and others.
Remember this
And know these words to be True:
"That all changes start from within
And all changes take place
More easily with Love."
So Love yourself and others
Then allow that which needs
To come into being.
"Evolve."

                                    Blessings to all.

8TH DECEMBER

First feel the Love in yourself
Then feel the anger and doubt.
Which is more comfortable?
Notice how your body experiences
Each separate emotion.
Surely it is better
To let Love
Flow through you
So that your entire body
Knows Peace and Harmony.
Then think
If this is how you react
What effect does your words and actions
Have on others?
So always consider Love.
Even after the event
It is never too late
To send Love
So that all
May enjoy and know
The untold Wisdom
Of Loving Kindness.

                              Blessings to all.

9TH DECEMBER

When all is in fast movement around you
Look to your very centre
For Stillness.
Such insight
Will bring the Truth
For how else will you understand
What is false or not?
If your centre cannot be found
Step back.
Hold within your mind
All possibilities
Then let time unravel them
Allowing that which is permanent
To remain.
Give Loving space
For only in this way
Can others find themselves
And all of life's patterns unfold.

Blessings to all.

10TH DECEMBER

Noise has become
Part of your daily life.
Yet for the most part
You do not hear it
For you have learnt not to listen
And in doing so
You have also forgotten
The Joy of Silence.
For it is there
In the Silence
That answers are found.
It is where True Love is given
And possibilities manifest themselves.
Therefore take time
To find the Stillness
That will lead into Silence
Allowing you to grow
And develop Understanding and Wisdom.

                                                  Blessings to all.

11TH DECEMBER

Let your day begin with Silence
And in that space
Give gratitude and Love
For another day.
In this way
All of your actions and thoughts
Will start from a place of Peace.
Even if your mind strays
It will be easier to return
And you can continue
Your daily activities
Knowing that you have done your best
To promote Loving Kindness in yourself
For it has been planted
In your Heart and Mind.
Therefore
If only for a moment
Remember to continue this practice
Letting Love flow through you
So that you may give freely to others.

Blessings to all.

12TH DECEMBER

From your tomorrows
Come your yesterdays.
Therefore take time to plan
Your actions and pathway.
Even if you cannot keep to them
There will at least be
The seed which has been sown.
By doing so
When the time is right
Changes will develop.
Know this to be true
So that you move slowly
Towards your goal
For such is the nature
Of your pathway
That you must observe all
Of your surroundings.
In doing so
Nothing is wasted.
Furthermore much can be gained.
Be awake and aware
Then you will know
That all will be given
At the right time.

Blessings to all.

13TH DECEMBER

Let your Light surround you
Then gently move forward
In its protective glow.
Feel yourself centered
So that at any instance
You may use that which is part of you.
Know that your Light
Will continue to shine
Even in your darkest hours.
Therefore sit quietly
Even if only for a moment
Knowing that this too will pass
Leaving you clear to go forward
And to once again
See and feel your Light.
Such is the way
Of all Creation
A giving and receiving
Being helped and helping others
With Love
Along life's pathway.

                                    Blessings to all.

14TH DECEMBER

Time waits for no man.
Yet time has been created by humans
To help them in their day.
Yet this is another example
Of how such inventions
Have turned against humankind.
What was once their friend
Is now their enemy
For they try to do so much
Before time runs out.
Yet time will always run out
For it is based on the planets
Which are constantly moving.
Therefore humankind should measure
Their life by their deeds
Thoughts and actions.
This should be the measurement of their day
Assessing how much has been done for others
And how much Loving Kindness
Has been added to their world.

Blessings to all.

15TH DECEMBER

Slow down.
Let time slip into a natural rhythm.
Allow yourself some Peace
And the chance to progress
At a gentler pace.
Let others pass you by
Knowing that each step you take
Is made with Love for all in mind.
In this way
You will know
That you have done your best
And helped to continue
The natural flow of events
Helping to restore order
Out of chaos
And bring harmony back
Into the lives
Of your fellow beings.
Walk with Peace and Love
Being a silent example to all.

Blessings to all.

16TH DECEMBER

Where do you search for Love?
Is it externally?
Or do you first
Look to give Love?
For most
Life begins
With an expression
Of outer Love
Thus forming an inner one.
It is at this time
That Inner Love develops
A bonding between parent and child.
Yet the former must let go of the latter
Or how else can they know
If their job has been completed?
For children must be strong enough
To stand on their own feet
So that they may in turn
Be strong enough
To support life themselves.
Therefore let your Love shine.
Ask for no rewards.
Hold no ties
Then all shall flow as it should.

Blessings to all.

17TH DECEMBER

Just as the summer winds blow
So there are changes developing.
Look no more to what was
But open your horizons
So that you are without limitation
For such are the changes
That you will be glad.
Be ever vigilant
For they shall occur.
And it is right to note
The exact time and circumstance
Thereby allowing
Greater Wisdom and Understanding
To assist you.
Be open.
Sit.
Be Still
For fruition is at hand.

Blessings to all.

18TH DECEMBER

Waiting for Peace
  Is not always right.
Steps need to be made
By passive individuals
So that Peace may spread to all.
For humankind has within themselves
The ability to change
Hearts and Minds.
Therefore by Loving actions
Show the alternative
To anger and hate.
By doing so
Others will feel the change
In the earthly vibrations
Allowing them the choice
To be frantic or calm
In their everyday activities.

                    Blessings to all.

19TH DECEMBER

Flowers blossom
Then they fade
And are gone.
Yet their roots may
Stay in the ground
To bloom the following year.
So it is with relationships.
If they were meant to last
Nothing will deter them
From enduring all weathers.
Through the rough and smooth
They will be a constant source
Of comfort and strength.
Therefore why worry or fret?
Let time take its own course.
Be open and Loving to all.
Allow each their own progression
Either to remain
Or to move on
Until you meet again.

Blessings to all.

20TH DECEMBER

When you truly let go
     There comes a blessed release
As if the heaviness
Of all of the years
Has been lifted.
The weight has at last gone.
All is Light and Balanced
And you feel free
To go onward
In your own way
At your own pace.
So look to the natural
Things of the world:
Flowers
Trees
Animals
The sky with its varied clouds.
Then seek a deeper Understanding
Of the pattern of all things
And there
Among the Order and Love
Of all Creation
You will find your place.

                              Blessings to all.

21ST DECEMBER

From within comes a great stream
A torrent of thought and feeling.
It is up to you to decipher
That which is worthwhile
From that which is not.
Therefore with each step
It is necessary
To access the information
That is given
To make use of that
Which has worth
And to disregard the rest.
In this way
With Understanding
You can build
On the foundation
Of your Inner Being
Going forward
In the Light of Love and Truth
And trusting your own decisions
Which is the way of perfect growth.

Blessings to all.

22ND DECEMBER

Love is a softening.
Love is a trusting.
Being able to give
Freely of oneself
Without thought
Of receiving anything in return.
It is a gentleness of Heart.
An acceptance
Of another's uniqueness
And a willingness
To allow space
Between you both
For in this space
You shall be joined together
In Love.

                              Blessings to all.

23RD DECEMBER

Words that come from the Heart
Hold true meaning
While words spoken in haste
Bring with them the ability to hurt.
Therefore it is important
For you to remember
This simple Truth:
"Once you have spoken
You can never take back
The imprint that you have made."
So wait.
Open your Heart
Then speak or not
For words should be used
To bring Love and healing
Or else not used at all.
Remember this adage
"Count to Ten."
This was spoken by a wise being.
So follow this
And if not spoken
Silently send Love to all
For this will bring Peace to those who need it.

Blessings to all.

24TH DECEMBER

The answer to any question
Is Love
For with Love
In your Heart
There can only be
The right outcome.
Think of Love
Imagine your body and mind
Filled with its energy.
Experience the reality of Love.
Notice the physical
And the mental changes.
Is this how you wish to be?
Then always revert back
To Love.
Even in difficult moments
Let Love be your guide
Allowing you
To move forward
In its rays of Light.

                                        Blessings to all.

25TH DECEMBER

Consider Love.
What does it mean to you?
Is it something that you hold onto?
Or is it shared
Given freely to others?
Do you talk of it
Or give silently?
Is it part of your life?
For when it is
There is a peaceful Silence within
Allowing you to be free from fear.
This will bring Harmony
Letting you soften and work from
A place of continuous Love.
You will expand your awareness
Being able to melt with the Universe
Thereby being a vessel of comfort to all.
Go with Love.
Become Love
And share the most precious Gift of all.

Blessings to all.

26TH DECEMBER

Sometimes you will forget
Everything that you have learnt.
Do not fret or worry
For it is easy to get caught up
In your everyday life.
Yet in order to live
A complete life
You must stop and re-remember
Who you really are.
So be still.
Listen to the rhythm of nature.
Tune into the pulse of the Universe
And you will be connected with the Truth
Which will allow you
To readjust yourself
Feeling calmer and at Peace.
This will allow you to go forward
Bringing Love to all
Including yourself.

Blessings to all.

27TH DECEMBER

Look no further than yourself
For in you is all that you need.
By going inwards
You will discover
Your True strength
And have the Trust
To allow it to expand.
Sit still.
Breathe gently.
Let your breath take you
Into your Still centre.
It is from there
That Self
Will radiate outward
Giving you the courage
To go forward
With Love and Compassion.
These attributes are the foundation of life.
So go quietly
Sending Love and Compassion
Silently to all.

Blessings to all.

28TH DECEMBER

Only Love endures
Hate eats away
The person hating.
Therefore choose Love.
Let this be your Gift
For all of Creation
For this is the purpose
Of existence.
Know this to be True:
"There is only Love.
It heals
And brings the ability
To create a world
Of Peace and Harmony.
All else passes."

                                    Blessings to all.

29TH DECEMBER

When we speak of self
We say I.
Yet there is a larger Self
And it is from there
That we begin to experience
The ability to create
A world of goodliness around
And within our own existence.
By doing so
The individual can
Bring into being
That which is required
For a life filled
With Peace and Harmony.
So what is the foundation
For such a life?
It is the blissful Energy
Of Loving Kindness.
Therefore practice
Until each breath and thought
Radiates the Light of Love.

Blessings to all.

30TH DECEMBER

As you have nearly reached
The end of your year
Can you look back
And see what changes if any
Have taken place?
Has your awareness moved on?
Do you see more of the Whole
And your place in it?
Or are you still centered from self?
Do you know where you are coming from?
Is it your Heart or your head
Or indeed a balanced
Mixture of both?
Does your Light shine within you
Or do you think
That it is a little ahead of you
Always looking for your Now?
Know these words to be True:
"By realizing that you live in the Now
You understand that you are your Now.
And in doing so
You can move forward
As a ray of Light and Love."

Blessings to all.

31ST DECEMBER

Life is made up of circles.
Look to the seasons:
See how there is a never-ending flow.
Look to time:
Days
Weeks
Years
Come and go in a continuous round.
And yet it is thought by some
That there is only one chance
To move towards perfection.
How can this be so?
Why should humans be outside
The natural rhythm?
Therefore be kind to yourself
For you are always given
Many chances.
At every moment
You can move
In a different direction.
So slowly and with Love and Light
Open your Heart
Which will bring
Peace and Contentment to you.

Blessings to all.

Lightning Source UK Ltd.
Milton Keynes UK
UKOW06f1903170915

258833UK00013B/174/P